breaking silence

The Story of Helen Keller for Kids

sarah michaels

contents

Introduction 5

1. EARLY LIFE 15
Birth and family 15
Early childhood 19

2. MEETING ANNE SULLIVAN 25
The arrival of Anne Sullivan 25
Initial challenges in communication 30
The breakthrough at the water pump 34

3. LEARNING AND GROWTH 39
Helen's education journey 39
Learning to read and write 44
Attending Perkins Institute for the Blind 48

4. COLLEGE YEARS 53
Helen's determination to attend college 53
Challenges faced and overcome 57
Graduation from Radcliffe College 62

5. ADVOCACY AND ACTIVISM 67
Helen's work as a public speaker 67
Advocacy for people with disabilities 71
Involvement in social and political causes 76

6. WRITING AND ACHIEVEMENTS 81
Helen's books and publications 81
Awards and recognitions 86
Influence on future generations 90

7. FRIENDSHIP AND SUPPORT 95
Relationship with Anne Sullivan 95
Other important figures in Helen's life 99
Community and network of supporters 103

8. LEGACY AND INSPIRATION 109

Fun Facts 115
Conclusion 121
Glossary 127
Resources 135

introduction

Imagine a world where you can't see the bright colors of a rainbow or hear the laughter of your friends. That was the world Helen Keller lived in. Born on June 27, 1880, in Tuscumbia, Alabama, Helen was a healthy baby who brought joy to her family. Her father, Arthur Keller, was a former Confederate Army captain, and her mother, Kate Keller, was known for her kindness and grace. They were delighted with their lively, curious little girl.

Everything changed when Helen was just 19 months old. She fell seriously ill with what doctors then called "brain fever." Today, we think it was probably scarlet fever or meningitis. The illness left Helen both blind and deaf. Suddenly, she was plunged into a silent, dark world, unable to understand what had happened to her or how to communicate her needs and feelings to those around her.

Helen's parents were heartbroken but determined to find a way to help her. Helen's mother read about the successful education of another deaf and blind girl and was inspired to seek similar help for her daughter. This led the Kellers to the Perkins Institute for the Blind in Boston, where they were introduced to Anne Sullivan, a young woman whose own struggles with vision problems had given her a special empathy and strength.

When Anne arrived at the Keller household in March 1887, she faced an enormous challenge. Helen, by then almost seven years old, was frustrated and unruly. She couldn't communicate effectively, and her inability to understand the world around her often led to tantrums. Anne knew she had to find a way to break through the barriers of darkness and silence.

One of the most famous moments in Helen's life happened just a month after Anne's arrival. Anne took Helen to a water pump outside the house. She pumped water over Helen's hand while spelling out the word "w-a-t-e-r" on her other palm. Suddenly, Helen made the connection. She understood that the cool liquid flowing over her hand was "water." This was her first real step into the world of language.

From that moment on, Helen's thirst for knowledge seemed unquenchable. She learned to spell more words, and with each new word, she discovered a new way to connect with the world around her. She didn't just learn names for objects; she began to understand concepts and ideas. Her world was no longer a dark, confusing place but one filled with possibilities.

Helen's progress was astounding. She quickly moved from spelling simple words to forming sentences and even learning to read Braille, a system of raised dots that represent letters and numbers, allowing blind people to read with their fingertips. Anne was by her side every step of the way, teaching her tirelessly and celebrating each new achievement.

Helen's education didn't stop there. She was determined to attend college, something that was almost unheard of for someone with her disabilities at the time. But Helen was not one to be deterred by societal expectations. With Anne's help, she prepared rigorously and was admitted to Radcliffe College, where she graduated cum laude in 1904.

During her time at Radcliffe, Helen wrote her autobiography, "The Story of My Life." In it, she detailed her early years, her relationship with Anne, and her educational journey. The book was an instant success, bringing Helen's incredible story to a wider audience and making her an inspirational figure worldwide.

But Helen didn't stop at being an author and a scholar. She dedicated her life to advocating for the rights of people with disabilities. She traveled the world, giving speeches and raising awareness about the challenges faced by those who are blind or deaf. She worked tirelessly with organizations like the American Foundation for the Blind, fighting for better opportunities and rights for people with disabilities.

Helen's activism extended beyond disability rights. She was also a vocal advocate for women's suffrage, labor rights, and social justice. She believed passionately in the power of education and equal opportunities for all people, regardless of their circumstances. Her advocacy work was recognized with numerous awards and honors, and she became a symbol of strength and determination.

One of the remarkable aspects of Helen's story is her enduring friendship with Anne Sullivan. Their relationship was based on mutual respect and love. Anne's teaching methods were innovative and patient, and her belief in Helen's potential never wavered. Even when Anne's own health began to fail, she continued to support Helen in every way she could.

After Anne Sullivan's death, Helen continued her work with the help of Polly Thomson, another dedicated companion and teacher. Together, they traveled extensively, and Helen's influence continued to grow. Her speeches and writings inspired countless people to overcome their own challenges and to strive for a better, more inclusive world.

significance and impact

Helen Keller broke down barriers that seemed impossible to overcome. Imagine being unable to see or hear, yet achieving things most people wouldn't dare to dream of. Helen did exactly that. She didn't just learn to communicate; she excelled at it. Her ability to connect with people despite her disabilities showed that limitations are often more about perception than reality.

One of Helen's most significant contributions was her role in changing public attitudes toward people with disabilities. Before Helen Keller, many people believed that those who were blind or deaf could not be educated or lead productive lives.

Helen shattered those misconceptions through her achievements. She proved that people with disabilities have the potential to learn, grow, and contribute to society just like anyone else.

Helen's education was a groundbreaking example of what could be achieved with the right support and resources. Her success at Radcliffe College, where she graduated with honors, sent a powerful message to the world: disability does not equal inability. This helped pave the way for future educational opportunities for people with disabilities, leading to more inclusive and accessible schools and universities.

Helen's work as an advocate for people with disabilities had a profound impact on public policy. She worked tirelessly with organizations like the American Foundation for the Blind to improve the lives of blind individuals. Her efforts contributed to the development of programs and laws that provided better education, job opportunities, and support services for people with disabilities.

Beyond her work with disability rights, Helen Keller was a passionate advocate for social justice. She believed in equality for all people, regardless of their background or circumstances. Helen spoke out for women's suffrage, arguing that women should have the right to vote and participate fully in society. She supported labor rights, standing up for fair wages and better working conditions for workers. Her activism extended to many areas, demonstrating her commitment to making the world a better place for everyone.

One of the most powerful aspects of Helen's story is her ability to inspire others. She showed that no matter what obstacles you face, you can achieve great things with perseverance and hard work. Helen became a role model for millions of people around the world, inspiring them to overcome their own challenges and strive for their dreams. Her speeches and writings continue to motivate people to this day.

Helen's legacy also includes her contributions to literature. She wrote numerous books and articles that shared her experiences and insights with the world. Her autobiography, "The Story of My Life," is still widely read and admired. Through her writing, Helen provided a firsthand account of what it was like to be both blind and deaf, offering valuable perspectives that have educated and enlightened many readers.

In addition to her literary works, Helen was a prolific speaker. Despite her disabilities, she traveled extensively, giving lectures and talks about her life and her beliefs. Her ability to communicate her message powerfully and effectively made her a sought-after speaker, and her presentations left lasting impressions on those who heard her.

Helen's impact can also be seen in the advancements in technology and resources for people with disabilities. Tools like Braille and sign language became more widely recognized and used thanks to Helen's advocacy. Today, there are numerous technologies and devices designed to assist people with disabilities, many of which owe their development to the awareness and demand created by Helen's work.

Helen Keller's influence reached beyond her own time. She laid the groundwork for future generations of activists and advocates. Her story continues to be a source of inspiration for people fighting for equality and justice in various fields. Her life's work has encouraged countless individuals to take up the cause of disability rights, ensuring that her legacy lives on through ongoing efforts to create a more inclusive and accessible world.

Helen's relationship with her teacher, Anne Sullivan, is another significant aspect of her story. Their partnership demonstrated the importance of mentorship and support in overcoming challenges. Anne's dedication and innovative teaching methods were crucial to Helen's success. Their bond showed that with the right guidance and encouragement, people can achieve remarkable things.

Even after Anne Sullivan's passing, Helen continued her work with the help of Polly Thomson and others. This continuity showed the importance of community and support networks in sustaining advocacy and achieving long-term goals. Helen's ability to inspire and rally people around her cause ensured that her work continued even when she was no longer able to lead it herself.

1 / early life

birth and family

HELEN KELLER'S story begins on June 27, 1880, in a small town called Tuscumbia in Alabama. She was born to a loving family who had no idea that their little girl would grow up to become one of the most remarkable women in history. Her parents, Arthur and Kate Keller, were thrilled when Helen arrived, bringing joy and excitement into their lives.

Arthur Keller, Helen's father, had a background that was steeped in Southern tradition. He had been a captain in the Confederate Army during the Civil War, which meant he had seen a lot of hardship and change in his life. After the war, he became the editor of a local newspaper, the "North

Alabamian." Arthur was known for his strong opinions and dedication to his work, qualities that would later influence Helen's own determination and drive.

Kate Keller, Helen's mother, was a kind and caring woman who came from a well-respected family. She was known for her grace and gentleness, and she adored her children. Kate's father, Charles Adams, was a prominent figure who had served as a brigadier general in the Confederate Army. This connection to a military past gave Helen's family a certain status in their community, but it also came with its own set of challenges.

The Kellers lived in a comfortable home called Ivy Green. Surrounded by beautiful gardens and orchards, Ivy Green was an idyllic place for a child to grow up. The house itself was a white, clapboard structure with wide porches and large, airy rooms. It was here that Helen took her first steps and uttered her first words, blissfully unaware of the struggles that lay ahead.

Helen was the first of five children in the Keller family. She had two younger brothers, James and William, and two younger sisters, Mildred and Phillips Brooks. As the oldest, Helen often took on a leadership role among her siblings, even though she herself was facing tremendous challenges.

From the beginning, Helen was a bright and curious child. She was always eager to explore her surroundings and learn new things. Her parents noticed early on that she had a keen sense of adventure. Whether it was crawling around the garden or playing with her family's dogs, Helen was full of energy and enthusiasm.

Tragedy struck when Helen was just 19 months old. She fell gravely ill with a fever that was likely scarlet fever or meningitis. The illness lasted several weeks, and when it finally passed, Helen's parents were relieved that their daughter had survived. But soon, they noticed something was terribly wrong. Helen no longer responded to sounds or sights. She had become both deaf and blind.

The sudden loss of her sight and hearing plunged Helen into a world of silence and darkness. For a while, she was a very frustrated and angry child. She couldn't understand why she couldn't communicate with her family or why they couldn't understand her. This led to many tantrums and fits of rage, which were heartbreaking for her parents to witness.

Despite these challenges, Helen's family was determined to help her. They loved her deeply and wanted her to have the best life possible. Kate, especially, was relentless in her search for ways to educate and communicate with Helen. She read about other children who had overcome similar challenges and sought advice from doctors and educators.

One such piece of advice led the Kellers to the Perkins Institute for the Blind in Boston. There, they found a teacher named Anne Sullivan, who would become one of the most important figures in Helen's life. Anne herself had faced significant challenges, having been nearly blind due to a severe eye infection. Her experiences gave her a unique perspective and a deep empathy for Helen's struggles.

When Anne arrived at Ivy Green, she immediately saw the potential in Helen. She believed that with the right guidance and patience, Helen could learn to communicate and thrive. Anne's arrival marked the beginning of a new chapter in Helen's life, one filled with hope and possibility.

Anne introduced Helen to the world of language using innovative methods that included spelling words into Helen's hand. The breakthrough moment came when Helen connected the feeling of water with the letters Anne was spelling out on her palm. This was a pivotal moment that opened up a whole new world for Helen.

Helen's relationship with her family, especially her parents, played a crucial role in her development. Their unwavering support and belief in her abilities gave Helen the confidence to push forward despite her disabilities. Arthur and Kate Keller might not have known how to help their daughter at first, but their determination to find a way made all the difference.

Helen's siblings also played an important role in her life. They grew up understanding her needs and finding ways to include her in their activities. Mildred, in particular, shared a close bond with Helen, and their relationship brought a lot of joy to both sisters.

The strong foundation of love and support that Helen received from her family helped her to overcome the many obstacles she faced. It was their belief in her potential that fueled her own belief in herself. This sense of security and encouragement was vital as Helen embarked on her incredible journey of learning and advocacy.

early childhood

As a baby, Helen was full of energy. She crawled around the house with boundless enthusiasm, and her laughter often filled the rooms. Her parents,

Arthur and Kate, delighted in her every milestone —her first steps, her first words, and the way she interacted with her surroundings. Helen's bright eyes seemed to take in everything, and she was quick to smile and giggle at the simplest of amusements.

Life for the Keller family was peaceful and content. Helen's father, Arthur, worked as an editor for the local newspaper, and her mother, Kate, took care of the household and the children. Helen was the firstborn, and her arrival brought immense joy to her parents. As she grew, it became clear that she was a curious and intelligent child, eager to explore the world around her.

Helen's favorite place to play was in the garden. She loved the feel of the grass under her feet and the scent of blooming flowers. She would often toddle around, touching the leaves and petals, fascinated by the textures and smells. The garden was her playground, and she would spend hours there, lost in her own little world of discovery.

But life took a dramatic turn when Helen was just 19 months old. One day, she fell seriously ill with a high fever. Her parents were deeply worried and called for the doctor. The illness was severe, and for several days, little Helen lay in bed, her body wracked with fever. Her mother and father stayed by her side, hoping and praying for her recovery.

The fever finally broke, and Helen began to recover physically. Her family was relieved, believing the worst was over. However, they soon noticed that something was terribly wrong. Helen no longer reacted to the familiar sounds of her mother's voice or the sight of her father's face. She seemed lost in a world of her own, unresponsive to the environment that she once found so captivating.

It became apparent that the illness had left Helen both blind and deaf. The joyful, curious child who had once delighted in exploring her garden was now unable to see the flowers or hear her parents' voices. This sudden change was devastating for the Keller family. They could hardly fathom the impact this would have on Helen's life and their own.

For Helen, the world had changed dramatically. The bright and colorful garden, the sounds of birds chirping, the rustling of leaves—all were gone. She was plunged into a silent, dark world that she couldn't understand. This new reality was confusing and frightening for her. Unable to communicate or understand what had happened, she often felt isolated and frustrated.

As the months passed, Helen's frustration grew. She couldn't express her needs or understand the world around her, leading to frequent tantrums and outbursts. Her parents were heartbroken, not knowing how to help their beloved daughter. They tried everything they could think of, but it seemed impossible to break through the barriers that her illness had created.

Despite the challenges, Helen's family never gave up on her. They were determined to find a way to reach her and help her navigate this new, dark world. Her mother, Kate, especially, was relentless in her search for answers. She read about other children with similar conditions and sought advice from doctors and educators, hoping to find a solution.

Helen's condition isolated her from the world, but it didn't extinguish her spirit. She still had that spark of curiosity and intelligence within her, even though she couldn't express it. Her family's love and dedication were crucial in keeping that spark alive. They provided her with as much comfort and normalcy as they could, trying to find ways to engage her and make her feel connected.

The turning point in Helen's life came when her parents learned about the Perkins Institute for the Blind in Boston. They read about the remarkable work being done there and decided to reach out for help. This decision led to the arrival of Anne Sullivan, a young teacher whose own experience with vision problems made her uniquely qualified to help Helen.

Anne Sullivan arrived at Ivy Green in March 1887, bringing with her a sense of hope and possibility. She immediately saw the potential in Helen and was determined to unlock it. Anne began by establishing a bond with Helen, understanding that trust and connection were essential before any real progress could be made.

Anne's innovative teaching methods started to make a difference. She introduced Helen to the concept of language using tactile sign language, spelling words into her hand. This approach slowly began to penetrate the dark and silent world Helen was trapped in. The breakthrough moment came with the word "water," opening the door to communication and understanding for Helen.

2 / meeting anne sullivan

the arrival of anne sullivan

ANNE SULLIVAN WAS no stranger to hardship. Born in 1866 to Irish immigrants, she lost her mother at a young age and was later abandoned by her father. Anne and her younger brother Jimmie were sent to live in a poorhouse, a place for destitute families. The conditions were harsh, and Jimmie, who was very ill, died a few months later. Anne herself suffered from severe eye problems, which left her nearly blind for much of her childhood.

Despite these challenges, Anne was determined to make something of her life. At the age of 14, she convinced a state inspector to send her to the Perkins Institute for the Blind in Boston. There, she underwent several surgeries that improved her vision and received an education. Anne's own experiences with blindness gave her a deep understanding of what Helen was going through, and her perseverance and resilience prepared her for the challenges ahead.

When Anne arrived at Ivy Green, she found a little girl who was intelligent but unruly, frustrated by her inability to communicate. Helen's wild tantrums and outbursts were her only way of expressing her frustration. Anne quickly realized that she needed to establish control and discipline while also building a bond of trust and love.

One of the first things Anne did was to give Helen a doll. This simple gift was more than just a toy; it was a tool for teaching. Anne used the doll to introduce Helen to the concept of language. She spelled out the word "d-o-l-l" into Helen's hand while allowing her to feel the letters. At first, Helen was puzzled and resisted the lessons, but Anne persisted.

To help Helen understand that everything had a name, Anne used a variety of objects around the house and spelled their names into Helen's hand. She also introduced the manual alphabet, a system of finger-spelling used by people who are deaf. Each letter had a specific hand shape, and Anne would place Helen's hand on her own to help her learn the shapes. This was the first step in bridging the gap between Helen and the world around her.

A breakthrough came one day at the water pump outside the house. Anne was pumping water over Helen's hand while spelling out "w-a-t-e-r" on her palm. Suddenly, Helen made the connection. She understood that the cool liquid flowing over her hand was "water." This realization was monumental. For the first time, Helen grasped that everything had a name, and she could learn to communicate those names.

This moment was a turning point in Helen's life. The concept of language had been unlocked, and Helen was eager to learn more. She began to ask for the names of everything around her, spelling out words into Anne's hand and eagerly waiting for the answers. This newfound ability to communicate opened up a whole new world for Helen. Her tantrums decreased, and her frustration turned into excitement and curiosity.

Anne's teaching methods were innovative and hands-on. She used everyday experiences and objects to teach Helen about the world. For example, she would take Helen to the garden and let her feel the different plants while spelling out their names. This multisensory approach helped Helen understand and remember the words she was learning. Anne also used a form of storytelling, describing objects and actions in vivid detail to help Helen form mental images.

As Helen's vocabulary grew, Anne introduced more complex concepts. She taught Helen about abstract ideas like love, happiness, and sadness by associating them with experiences Helen could relate to. For instance, Anne would hug Helen tightly and spell "love" into her hand, helping her associate the feeling of being hugged with the concept of love. This method of teaching abstract concepts through tangible experiences was crucial in Helen's understanding of the world.

Anne's role in Helen's life extended beyond that of a teacher. She became a mentor, a friend, and a constant source of support. Their relationship was built on mutual respect and affection, which allowed Helen to thrive. Anne's patience and dedication were unwavering, even when faced with the challenges of Helen's stubbornness and occasional resistance.

One of the most remarkable aspects of Anne's teaching was her insistence on treating Helen as an intelligent and capable individual. She never underestimated Helen's abilities or let her disabilities define her. This belief in Helen's potential was instrumental in Helen's development and achievements. Anne's high expectations and unwavering support empowered Helen to push her own boundaries and strive for greatness.

As Helen continued to learn, Anne introduced her to reading and writing using Braille, a system of raised dots that represent letters and numbers. Helen quickly became proficient in Braille, allowing her to read books and further expand her knowledge. Anne also taught Helen how to write using a special board that helped her form letters correctly. These skills were essential for Helen's academic success and future career as a writer and speaker.

The relationship between Anne and Helen was not without its challenges. There were times when Helen's frustrations resurfaced, and she would resist Anne's lessons. Anne, however, was steadfast in her commitment. She adapted her teaching methods to suit Helen's needs and found creative ways to keep her engaged and motivated. This adaptability and persistence were key factors in Helen's continued progress.

initial challenges in communication

From the start, Anne faced a significant hurdle: Helen's lack of discipline. Accustomed to getting her way through tantrums and physical outbursts, Helen had little patience for lessons or structured activities. Anne realized that before she could teach Helen anything, she needed to establish boundaries and a sense of order. This was no easy task. Helen was strong-willed and resistant to change.

Anne began by insisting on consistent routines and manners. For instance, she refused to let Helen eat with her hands or throw tantrums to get what she wanted. At first, this approach led to more outbursts, but Anne remained firm. Gradually, Helen started to understand that she couldn't simply act out to get her way. This newfound sense of discipline was crucial in preparing Helen for the lessons to come.

Next, Anne needed to find a way to communicate with Helen. She chose to use the manual alphabet, a system where each letter is represented by a different hand sign. Anne would spell out words by forming these signs into Helen's hand. Initially, this was a confusing and frustrating experience for Helen. She had no context for understanding that these signs represented words and ideas.

One of the first major challenges was getting Helen to associate the finger-spelled words with the objects they represented. For example, Anne would spell "d-o-l-l" while giving Helen a doll to hold. But without a clear understanding of what was happening, Helen often became frustrated and uninterested. Anne had to be patient and creative, finding ways to make the lessons engaging and meaningful.

A significant breakthrough came when Anne realized she needed to make the learning process more dynamic and multisensory. Instead of just spelling words into Helen's hand, Anne began using tactile experiences to reinforce the lessons. For instance, she would let Helen feel the water while spelling "w-a-t-e-r" or hold a flower while spelling "f-l-o-w-e-r." This method helped Helen make the connection between the spelled words and the objects they represented.

Despite these creative approaches, progress was slow. Helen's frustration would often boil over, leading to more tantrums and resistance. Anne had to balance firmness with compassion, understanding that Helen's outbursts were a result of her inability to communicate rather than disobedience.

Every small victory in understanding was met with setbacks, but Anne's unwavering dedication kept them moving forward.

One of the most challenging aspects of these initial lessons was teaching Helen about abstract concepts. Concrete objects like dolls and water were one thing, but how do you explain ideas like love, fear, or happiness to someone who can't see or hear? Anne tackled this by associating these concepts with physical experiences. For instance, she would give Helen a hug while spelling out "l-o-v-e" or create a playful atmosphere while spelling "h-a-p-p-y." These associations helped Helen grasp the meanings of these abstract ideas over time.

Another significant challenge was Helen's short attention span. Like any child, she would become easily distracted or bored. Anne had to find ways to keep her engaged. She incorporated games and play into the lessons, turning learning into an adventure. For example, she might hide objects around the garden for Helen to find, spelling out their names as she discovered them. This made learning exciting and interactive, holding Helen's attention longer.

As Helen began to understand more words, Anne introduced her to reading and writing using Braille. This system of raised dots allowed Helen to read with her fingertips. Learning Braille was another challenge. It required patience and precision, but Helen's eagerness to learn kept her motivated. Anne used a hands-on approach, guiding Helen's fingers over the Braille letters and words repeatedly until she could recognize them on her own.

One of the pivotal moments in Helen's early education was when she finally understood that everything had a name and that these names could be spelled out into her hand. This realization opened up a new world for her. She became a voracious learner, constantly asking for the names of objects around her. Her vocabulary expanded rapidly, and with it, her ability to communicate more effectively.

Anne also had to deal with the challenge of teaching Helen to write. This required special tools, such as a writing board that helped Helen form letters correctly. Writing was a painstaking process for Helen, but Anne's encouragement and patience made all the difference. Helen practiced diligently, and over time, her writing skills improved significantly.

Throughout these early challenges, the bond between Helen and Anne grew stronger. They developed a deep sense of trust and mutual respect. Anne's belief in Helen's potential never wavered, and this faith was instrumental in Helen's progress. Knowing that Anne believed in her gave Helen the confidence to tackle each new challenge with determination.

the breakthrough at the water pump

Helen was a curious and intelligent child, but the frustration of being unable to communicate had often led to tantrums and tears. Anne knew that Helen had the potential to understand language, but she needed to find a way to make that connection clear and tangible. Anne had tried various methods, spelling out words into Helen's hand while associating them with objects. But despite these efforts, the true meaning of these spelled words had not yet clicked for Helen.

On that spring day in 1887, Anne decided to take Helen outside to the well-house. It was a bright and warm day, the kind that made everything feel possible. Anne led Helen to the water pump, a familiar place where Helen loved to play with the water. Helen's love for water was one of the few pleasures she had left, and Anne decided to use this to her advantage.

Anne placed Helen's hand under the spout of

the pump and began to pump the handle, letting cool water gush over Helen's small hand. As the water flowed, Anne took Helen's other hand and began to spell out the word "w-a-t-e-r" into her palm. She repeated this several times, carefully and deliberately.

At first, it seemed like just another lesson, similar to the many they had gone through before. Helen felt the water and felt Anne's fingers moving in her palm, but the connection still eluded her. Anne didn't give up. She kept pumping the water, spelling "w-a-t-e-r" over and over again, hoping that something would click.

Then, it happened. Helen suddenly paused, a look of intense concentration crossing her face. Her hand, which had been feeling the water, stilled for a moment. It was as if a light had turned on in her mind. She stopped, and then she pulled her hand back and touched the ground, her way of asking for confirmation.

Anne spelled "w-a-t-e-r" again, and this time, Helen's face lit up with recognition. The cool liquid flowing over her hand had a name! The realization hit her like a bolt of lightning. Helen understood that the movements Anne was making in her hand represented the word "water." This was not just a random series of finger movements; it was communication. It was language.

The world opened up for Helen in that moment. She quickly began to ask for the names of other objects around her, eager to learn. Anne led her around the yard, spelling out the names of different things: "g-r-o-u-n-d," "p-u-m-p," "f-l-o-w-e-r." Each time, Helen's excitement grew as she grasped the concept that everything had a name, and these names could be learned through the patterns spelled into her hand.

The breakthrough at the water pump was monumental. It marked the beginning of Helen's journey into language and communication. She now had the key to unlock the world around her. The frustration and isolation she had felt began to melt away, replaced by a newfound sense of understanding and connection.

Helen's excitement was palpable. She wanted to learn the names of everything she touched. Anne could barely keep up with her rapid questions, but she was overjoyed by Helen's enthusiasm. This moment was what Anne had been working towards, and seeing Helen's joy and curiosity was the greatest reward.

The impact of this breakthrough was immediate

and profound. Helen's behavior changed dramatically. The tantrums and outbursts that had been so frequent became less common as she found new ways to express herself. She no longer felt as isolated and frustrated. The ability to communicate, even in this basic form, was liberating for her.

Helen's family was astonished by the change. They had watched her struggle for years, and now, in a single moment, everything was different. They saw Helen's transformation and were filled with hope for her future. Anne's success with Helen also reaffirmed their decision to bring her into their home. They realized that Anne's unconventional methods were exactly what Helen needed.

This breakthrough was just the beginning. With the door to language now open, Helen's learning accelerated rapidly. She absorbed new words with incredible speed, and Anne continued to build on this foundation, introducing more complex concepts and expanding Helen's understanding of the world.

Anne's teaching went beyond simple vocabulary. She taught Helen about the world around her, using hands-on experiences and tactile learning. They would go for walks, and Anne would describe the environment, spelling out words for the things they encountered. This method helped Helen form a mental map of her surroundings and understand how everything was interconnected.

3 / learning and growth

helen's education journey

AFTER THE PIVOTAL moment at the water pump, Helen's thirst for knowledge grew insatiable. She wanted to know the name of everything she touched, saw, or heard about. Anne Sullivan, affectionately known as "Teacher" by Helen, was more than ready to quench this thirst. She devised creative and engaging methods to teach Helen new concepts and words, turning everyday experiences into learning opportunities.

One of the first significant steps in Helen's education was learning to read. Anne introduced Helen to Braille, a system of raised dots that represent letters and numbers, allowing blind individuals to read through touch. Learning Braille was a meticulous process that required patience and persistence. Anne would guide Helen's fingers over the Braille characters, helping her recognize and memorize the patterns.

Helen quickly grasped the concept of Braille and was soon reading simple books. This newfound ability to read opened up an entirely new world for her. She could now access stories, poems, and information independently, which fueled her curiosity even further. Reading became one of Helen's greatest joys, and she devoured every book she could get her hands on.

Writing was another crucial skill that Helen needed to master. Anne taught her to write using a special board with grooves to guide her hand. Helen practiced tirelessly, forming letters and words until she could write legibly. Writing allowed Helen to express her thoughts and ideas more clearly, giving her a new way to communicate with the world.

Helen's education wasn't confined to reading and writing. Anne believed in a well-rounded education that included math, science, history, and geography. Teaching these subjects to a child who couldn't see or hear was no small feat, but Anne's innovative methods made it possible. For example, she used physical objects like beads and blocks to teach Helen basic math concepts, helping her understand numbers and arithmetic.

To teach history and geography, Anne used tactile maps and models. She would trace the outlines of countries, rivers, and mountains on Helen's hand, helping her form a mental picture of the world. These hands-on experiences made abstract concepts more concrete and understandable for Helen.

Science lessons were particularly exciting. Anne would take Helen on nature walks, describing the plants, animals, and natural phenomena they encountered. She spelled out the names of different species and explained their characteristics. Helen would feel the texture of leaves, the bark of trees, and the softness of petals, learning about the natural world through touch and smell.

As Helen's understanding grew, Anne introduced more complex subjects. She taught Helen about different cultures, famous historical figures, and significant events. These lessons were not just about memorizing facts but about understanding the broader context of human history and society.

Anne also encouraged Helen to pursue her

interests and passions. Helen developed a love for literature, particularly poetry. She admired poets like John Greenleaf Whittier and loved reading their works in Braille. Helen's passion for literature eventually led her to write her own stories and poems, expressing her thoughts and emotions in beautiful, evocative language.

Music was another area that fascinated Helen. Despite her inability to hear, she could feel the vibrations of musical instruments and appreciate the rhythms and patterns. Anne introduced her to famous composers and described their music, allowing Helen to develop a deep appreciation for the art form.

As Helen progressed in her studies, it became clear that she had an exceptional mind. Anne realized that Helen needed more advanced educational opportunities to fulfill her potential. This led to the decision to send Helen to the Perkins Institute for the Blind in Boston, the same school where Anne had been educated.

At Perkins, Helen had access to a broader range of resources and could interact with other students. This environment provided new challenges and learning experiences. Helen thrived at Perkins, excelling in her studies and forming lifelong friendships with her classmates.

One of Helen's most significant educational milestones was her decision to attend college. This was a bold and unprecedented move for someone with her disabilities. Helen set her sights on Radcliffe College, the women's counterpart to Harvard University. Preparing for college was an enormous undertaking that required rigorous study and intense focus.

Helen's admission to Radcliffe was a historic moment. She was the first deaf-blind person to attend the prestigious institution. Her time at Radcliffe was demanding but rewarding. She studied a wide range of subjects, from literature and philosophy to mathematics and history. Despite the challenges, Helen excelled academically, graduating with honors in 1904.

Throughout her college years, Anne remained by Helen's side, spelling out lectures and reading materials into her hand. Their partnership was a testament to the power of perseverance, dedication, and the unbreakable bond they shared. Anne's unwavering support and Helen's relentless determination enabled her to overcome the barriers that stood in her way.

learning to read and write

Anne Sullivan, Helen's dedicated teacher, knew that reading and writing were essential skills for Helen's growth and independence. She introduced Helen to Braille, a system of raised dots that represents letters and numbers, allowing blind individuals to read through touch. The invention of Braille was a game-changer for people with visual impairments, and for Helen, it was the key to unlocking a treasure trove of knowledge.

Learning Braille required patience and persistence. Anne began by teaching Helen the Braille alphabet. Each letter is represented by a unique arrangement of up to six dots within a cell. Helen used her fingertips to feel these dots and memorize their patterns. At first, it was challenging. Helen's fingers had to become accustomed to distinguishing the subtle differences between the dots, but her determination never wavered.

Anne made the lessons engaging by connecting them to Helen's interests. For instance, Helen loved stories, so Anne would read to her in Braille, helping her understand how the dots formed words and sentences. This multisensory approach made learning Braille an exciting adventure rather than a tedious task.

One of the first books Helen read in Braille was "The Frost King," a story about the changing seasons. The experience of reading a story independently was exhilarating for Helen. She could now dive into different worlds and explore new ideas through books. This newfound ability to read brought her immense joy and opened up endless possibilities for learning.

Writing was another important skill that Anne introduced to Helen. To help Helen write, Anne used a special writing board with grooves that guided Helen's hand, ensuring that her letters were formed correctly. Helen practiced tirelessly, forming each letter with care. Writing allowed Helen to express her thoughts and feelings in a tangible way, bridging the gap between her inner world and the people around her.

One of Helen's earliest writing tools was a grooved board that held a sheet of paper in place. Anne would guide Helen's hand to form letters and words. Initially, it was a slow and painstaking process. Helen had to learn the correct pressure to apply and how to move her hand smoothly across the paper. But with each practice session, her confidence and proficiency grew.

Anne also introduced Helen to a Braille typewriter, a device that enabled her to write more efficiently. The typewriter had six keys, each corresponding to one of the six dots in a Braille cell. By pressing different combinations of these keys, Helen could type out Braille characters. This tool was incredibly empowering for Helen, giving her the ability to write longer passages and even letters.

Helen's first letter was to Michael Anagnos, the director of the Perkins Institute for the Blind, who had supported her education. The letter was a heartfelt thank you, expressing her gratitude for his support. Writing this letter was a significant milestone for Helen, demonstrating her progress and the impact of Anne's teaching.

As Helen's reading and writing skills improved, Anne introduced her to more advanced materials. Helen read classic literature, poetry, and scientific texts in Braille, broadening her horizons and deepening her understanding of the world. Her favorite authors included Charles Dickens and William Shakespeare, whose works she read voraciously.

Helen's love for poetry blossomed during this time. She admired poets like John Greenleaf Whittier and Henry Wadsworth Longfellow. Their rhythmic verses and vivid imagery captivated her, inspiring her to write her own poems. Writing poetry became a way for Helen to express her emotions and share her unique perspective with the world.

One of Helen's early poems was titled "The Frost King," a tribute to the story she had read in Braille. Her poem reflected her deep appreciation for nature and the changing seasons. Writing poetry allowed Helen to explore her creativity and articulate her thoughts in a beautiful, lyrical form.

As Helen's proficiency in reading and writing grew, so did her desire to share her story with others. With Anne's guidance, she began working on her autobiography, "The Story of My Life." Writing her autobiography was a monumental task, requiring Helen to reflect on her experiences and articulate them in a way that others could understand. The process was challenging but deeply rewarding.

In her autobiography, Helen described her early childhood, the illness that left her blind and deaf, and the breakthrough at the water pump. She also wrote about her education journey, her relationship with Anne Sullivan, and the incredible impact of learning to read and write. "The Story of My Life" became an instant success, inspiring readers around the world with Helen's resilience and determination.

Helen's ability to read and write not only

enriched her own life but also paved the way for her to become a powerful advocate for people with disabilities. She used her writing to raise awareness about the challenges faced by individuals who are blind or deaf, advocating for better education, employment opportunities, and social inclusion.

attending perkins institute for the blind

Helen was both excited and nervous about attending Perkins. It meant leaving her familiar surroundings at Ivy Green and stepping into a new environment filled with other children who also had visual impairments. However, the prospect of new experiences and the chance to learn more was thrilling for her. She was eager to meet her peers and immerse herself in the rich educational opportunities that Perkins offered.

The journey to Boston, where Perkins was located, was an adventure in itself. Helen had never traveled so far from home before. She and Anne Sullivan embarked on the trip with a mixture of excitement and anticipation. Upon their arrival, they were greeted warmly by the staff and students at Perkins. Helen quickly felt at home in this community of learners who, like her, faced significant challenges but were determined to overcome them.

One of the first things that struck Helen about Perkins was the sense of camaraderie among the students. She met other children who were blind or visually impaired and realized that she was not alone in her experiences. This sense of belonging was incredibly comforting and empowering. Helen made friends who understood her struggles and shared her passion for learning. These friendships were a source of support and inspiration throughout her time at Perkins.

The academic curriculum at Perkins was rigorous and comprehensive. Helen studied a wide range of subjects, including literature, history, mathematics, and science. Each subject was taught using methods adapted for students with visual impairments. For example, literature classes involved reading Braille books and discussing them with teachers and peers. History lessons were brought to life through tactile maps and models, allowing Helen to visualize historical events and places.

Mathematics was another area where Helen excelled. Anne and the teachers at Perkins used a variety of tactile tools to teach mathematical concepts. Helen learned to solve complex problems using an abacus and other hands-on methods. She enjoyed the logical structure of mathematics and the challenge of solving intricate equations. Her ability to grasp these concepts demonstrated her intellectual prowess and determination to succeed.

Science was perhaps one of Helen's favorite subjects. She loved exploring the natural world and understanding how things worked. The teachers at Perkins encouraged this curiosity by incorporating hands-on experiments and nature walks into the curriculum. Helen studied biology by examining plants and animals through touch and smell. She learned about chemistry through safe, tactile experiments that demonstrated basic principles. These experiences deepened her appreciation for the natural world and fueled her desire to learn more.

One of the most remarkable aspects of Helen's education at Perkins was the individualized attention she received. The teachers understood her unique needs and adapted their methods accordingly. Anne Sullivan continued to play a crucial role in Helen's education, working closely with the teachers to ensure that Helen received the best possible instruction. This personalized approach allowed Helen to thrive academically and socially.

Perkins also emphasized the importance of extracurricular activities. Helen participated in various clubs and organizations, which helped her develop new skills and interests. She joined the literary club, where she had the opportunity to share her writings and listen to the works of her peers. This experience honed her writing abilities and gave her the confidence to express herself creatively.

Helen also became involved in music at Perkins. Despite her inability to hear, she could feel the vibrations of musical instruments and understand rhythm and melody through touch. She learned to play the piano, using her sense of touch to guide her fingers across the keys. Music became another way for Helen to connect with the world and express her emotions.

One of the most transformative experiences for Helen at Perkins was the exposure to a broader world of ideas and possibilities. The school frequently hosted guest speakers and visitors who shared their knowledge and experiences. Helen had the opportunity to meet influential figures, including Alexander Graham Bell, who had a profound impact on her understanding of communication and technology. These interactions broadened Helen's horizons and inspired her to think about how she could contribute to society.

Helen's time at Perkins was not without its challenges. She faced moments of frustration and self-doubt, particularly when grappling with difficult subjects or adapting to new methods of learning. However, the supportive environment at Perkins, combined with Anne's unwavering encouragement, helped her persevere. Helen learned the value of resilience and the importance of embracing challenges as opportunities for growth.

4 / college years

helen's determination to attend college

HELEN'S DESIRE TO attend college was fueled by her love for literature, history, and philosophy. She had been introduced to the works of great authors and thinkers at Perkins, and she wanted to delve deeper into these subjects. Helen dreamed of walking the halls of a prestigious university, sitting in lectures, and engaging in intellectual debates. She knew that a college education would not only broaden her horizons but also empower her to advocate more effectively for the rights of people with disabilities.

Anne Sullivan, Helen's devoted teacher and constant companion, fully supported Helen's dream. Anne understood the challenges that lay ahead but believed in Helen's potential. Together, they began preparing for the arduous journey to college. The first step was finding a suitable institution that would accommodate Helen's needs and provide her with the education she desired.

Helen set her sights on Radcliffe College, the women's counterpart to Harvard University. Radcliffe had a reputation for academic excellence and intellectual rigor, making it the perfect fit for Helen's ambitions. However, gaining admission to such a prestigious institution was no easy feat, especially for someone with Helen's disabilities. The entrance exams and academic requirements were rigorous, and Helen would need to prove her ability to succeed in a demanding academic environment.

Preparation for the entrance exams was intense. Helen and Anne spent countless hours studying together, covering subjects ranging from literature and history to mathematics and science. Anne read textbooks and literary works aloud to Helen, spelling out the words into her hand using the manual alphabet. Helen absorbed the information with remarkable speed and comprehension, driven by her determination to succeed.

The challenge of preparing for college was

compounded by the lack of resources available to students with disabilities at the time. There were no specialized textbooks in Braille, no accessible classrooms, and no accommodations for taking exams. Helen and Anne had to be creative and resourceful, finding ways to overcome these obstacles. Anne would often transcribe textbooks into Braille for Helen, painstakingly typing out each page so that Helen could study independently.

Despite the challenges, Helen remained undeterred. Her determination and hard work paid off when she was accepted to Radcliffe College in 1900. This achievement was historic, making Helen the first deaf-blind person to attend the prestigious institution. Her acceptance was a testament to her intellectual abilities and the groundbreaking progress she had made with Anne's guidance.

Helen's time at Radcliffe was both exhilarating and demanding. The academic rigor was intense, and Helen faced the additional challenge of navigating an environment not designed for someone with her disabilities. Lectures were particularly challenging, as there were no sign language interpreters or accessible notes. To overcome this, Anne sat beside Helen in every class, spelling out the lectures into her hand and taking detailed notes for her to review later.

Despite these difficulties, Helen thrived at Radcliffe. She immersed herself in her studies, relishing the opportunity to engage with complex ideas and contribute to intellectual discussions. Her favorite subjects included literature, philosophy, and history. She particularly enjoyed studying the works of great philosophers like Immanuel Kant and Plato, finding their ideas both challenging and inspiring.

Helen's determination to succeed at Radcliffe extended beyond academics. She was actively involved in campus life, participating in various clubs and organizations. She formed friendships with her classmates, who admired her perseverance and intellect. These relationships enriched her college experience, providing her with a sense of community and belonging.

One of the most remarkable aspects of Helen's college journey was her ability to write. She continued to hone her writing skills, producing essays, articles, and even poetry. Her writing was eloquent and insightful, reflecting her deep understanding of the subjects she studied. Helen's ability to articulate her thoughts so beautifully in writing was a powerful testament to her intellectual and creative abilities.

During her time at Radcliffe, Helen also worked

on her autobiography, "The Story of My Life." This book, which she had begun writing during her preparation for college, detailed her early years, her education journey, and the breakthrough moments that had shaped her life. Writing her autobiography was a deeply personal and reflective process, allowing Helen to share her experiences and inspire others with her story.

Helen's achievements at Radcliffe were celebrated widely. She graduated cum laude in 1904, a remarkable accomplishment that garnered admiration and respect from people around the world. Her success at Radcliffe demonstrated that with determination, support, and perseverance, even the most daunting challenges could be overcome. Helen's journey to and through college paved the way for future generations of students with disabilities, proving that higher education was within their reach.

challenges faced and overcome

One of the earliest and most significant challenges was the public perception of people with disabilities. During Helen's time, there was a widespread belief that individuals who were blind or deaf were incapable of leading productive lives. This societal bias often translated into limited opportunities for education and employment. Helen's decision to attend college was met with skepticism by many who doubted her ability to succeed in such a demanding environment. Despite these doubts, Helen was determined to prove that people with disabilities could achieve great things.

Attending Radcliffe College was an extraordinary achievement, but it also presented a unique set of challenges. The academic rigor of Radcliffe required Helen to keep up with her peers in an environment that was not designed to accommodate her needs. One of the most significant hurdles was accessing the course materials. At the time, there were no digital books or audiobooks, and very few textbooks were available in Braille. This meant that Anne Sullivan had to read the books aloud to Helen, spelling out each word into her hand using the manual alphabet.

This method of learning was incredibly time-consuming. Anne and Helen would spend countless hours each day going through the assigned readings. Anne's dedication was unwavering, but the process was mentally and physically exhausting for both of them. Despite these difficulties, Helen absorbed the information with remarkable speed and understanding. Her ability to retain and comprehend such vast amounts of material was a testament to her intellectual abilities and determination.

Taking exams was another significant challenge. Helen had to find a way to demonstrate her knowledge without the ability to write in a traditional manner. For written exams, she often used a typewriter, but even this had its limitations. Sometimes, Anne would act as a scribe, writing down Helen's answers as she spelled them out. This required a high level of coordination and trust between them. Despite these obstacles, Helen consistently performed well in her exams, proving her academic capabilities.

Social integration was also a challenge for Helen. While she was welcomed by her classmates and formed meaningful friendships, communication barriers sometimes made it difficult for her to participate fully in social activities. Conversations that flowed naturally for others required more effort and patience for Helen. However, she never let these barriers stop her from engaging with her peers. Her friends admired her perseverance and intelligence, and their support helped her navigate the social aspects of college life.

Beyond the academic and social challenges, Helen also faced personal struggles. The intense pressure to succeed and the constant scrutiny she was under could be overwhelming. There were times when Helen felt discouraged and doubted her own abilities. During these moments, Anne's support was crucial. Anne not only served as Helen's teacher and interpreter but also as her confidante and emotional anchor. She provided the encouragement and reassurance Helen needed to keep going.

Helen's determination to overcome these challenges was driven by her broader goals. She wanted to be an advocate for people with disabilities and to demonstrate that they could lead fulfilling and successful lives. Her success at Radcliffe was not just a personal triumph but a powerful statement to the world. Helen's achievements challenged societal prejudices and paved the way for future generations of students with disabilities.

Another significant challenge Helen faced was the physical and mental toll of her rigorous schedule. Balancing a demanding academic workload with the physical strain of learning through touch and sound required immense stamina. Helen often pushed herself to the brink of exhaustion, driven by her desire to succeed. Anne was always there to help manage her workload and ensure she took care of her health, but the demands of college life were relentless.

Despite these challenges, Helen's time at Radcliffe was filled with moments of joy and accomplishment. She loved learning and thrived in the intellectual environment. Each successful exam, each paper completed, and each new concept mastered was a victory that reinforced her belief in her own capabilities. Helen's resilience in the face of adversity inspired her classmates and professors alike.

Helen's journey also involved overcoming societal barriers outside of the academic world. She became an active advocate for people with disabilities, using her own experiences to highlight the need for better educational opportunities and support systems. Her public speeches and writings were influential in changing public perceptions and promoting legislative changes. Helen's advocacy work was a vital part of her legacy, demonstrating that her impact extended far beyond her own personal achievements.

One of the most profound challenges Helen faced was the ongoing battle against isolation. Despite her successes and the support of her friends and family, there were moments when the barriers of silence and darkness felt insurmountable. Yet, Helen always found a way to connect with the world around her, whether through her writing, her advocacy, or her close relationships. These connections were her lifeline, providing her with the strength to keep moving forward.

graduation from radcliffe college

The campus buzzed with excitement as students, faculty, and families gathered for the graduation ceremony. The air was filled with the scent of blooming flowers and the hum of conversations, creating an atmosphere of anticipation and celebration. For Helen, this day represented not just an academic achievement, but a powerful statement to the world about the capabilities of individuals with disabilities.

Helen's journey through Radcliffe had been anything but typical. She had navigated the rigorous academic environment with the help of Anne, who had become an integral part of her educational experience. Anne had tirelessly spelled out lectures, transcribed textbooks into Braille, and supported Helen through every exam and paper. Their partnership had become a symbol of the transformative power of dedication and innovation in education.

As Helen prepared for the ceremony, she reflected on the challenges she had overcome to reach this point. She remembered the long hours of studying, the late nights spent deciphering complex texts, and the moments of doubt when the workload seemed insurmountable. Each obstacle had tested her resolve, but she had emerged stronger and more determined each time.

The ceremony was held in the grand hall of Radcliffe, a space filled with history and tradition. Graduates sat in their caps and gowns, a sea of black robes and bright smiles. Helen took her place among them, her heart swelling with pride and gratitude. She could feel the presence of Anne beside her, a comforting and familiar presence that had been her guiding light throughout her academic journey.

The commencement address was delivered by a prominent figure in education, who spoke about the power of perseverance and the importance of lifelong learning. Helen listened intently, her fingers resting gently on Anne's hand as she spelled out the words. The speech resonated deeply with her, echoing the very principles that had guided her own path.

When it was time for the graduates to receive their diplomas, the room erupted in applause.

Helen's name was called, and she made her way to the stage with Anne by her side. As she accepted her diploma, the audience rose to their feet in a standing ovation. The applause was not just for Helen's academic achievements, but for the barriers she had broken and the inspiration she had become.

The moment was overwhelming. Helen felt a surge of emotions – pride, joy, and a deep sense of accomplishment. She had defied expectations and demonstrated that with determination and support, anything was possible. The diploma in her hand was more than a piece of paper; it was a testament to her hard work, resilience, and the power of education to transform lives.

After the ceremony, Helen and Anne were surrounded by well-wishers. Friends, family, and faculty members came to congratulate them, each one expressing their admiration for Helen's achievements. Among them was Alexander Graham Bell, a long-time supporter and friend, who had played a pivotal role in Helen's education. His presence was a reminder of the many people who had believed in her and supported her journey.

The celebration continued with a reception in the college courtyard. Tables were laden with food and drinks, and the sound of laughter filled the air. Helen reveled in the festivities, enjoying the company of her friends and the sense of camaraderie that had defined her time at Radcliffe. She felt a profound sense of belonging, knowing that she was part of a community that valued knowledge, innovation, and the pursuit of excellence.

As the day drew to a close, Helen and Anne took a moment to reflect on their journey. They found a quiet spot in the garden, away from the hustle and bustle of the celebration. The garden was a place of tranquility, where they could speak freely and share their thoughts. Helen expressed her gratitude to Anne, acknowledging the immense role she had played in her success. Anne, in turn, praised Helen's determination and intellect, marveling at how far they had come together.

The bond between Helen and Anne was unbreakable, forged through years of shared challenges and triumphs. Their partnership was a testament to the power of education and the impact that a dedicated teacher can have on a student's life. Anne had not only taught Helen academic subjects but had also instilled in her a love for learning and a belief in her own potential.

Graduating from Radcliffe was not the end of Helen's journey; it was a new beginning. With her diploma in hand, she was ready to embark on the next chapter of her life. She was determined to use her education to make a difference in the world, to advocate for the rights of people with disabilities, and to continue her pursuit of knowledge.

5 / advocacy and activism

helen's work as a public speaker

HELEN'S ENTRANCE into public speaking began shortly after her graduation. She was invited to speak at various events, from small gatherings to large conferences. Her first major speaking engagement was at a fundraiser for the American Foundation for the Blind (AFB), an organization she would remain deeply involved with throughout her life. Helen's speech was a resounding success. Her eloquence, passion, and ability to connect with her audience left a lasting impression.

Helen's public speaking engagements were often centered around her personal experiences and the challenges she had overcome. She spoke candidly about the obstacles she faced as a deaf-blind person and how education and support had transformed her life. Her story resonated with audiences, highlighting the importance of providing opportunities and resources for people with disabilities.

One of Helen's most powerful speeches was delivered at Carnegie Hall in New York City. The grand hall was filled to capacity, with people eager to hear from the woman who had defied so many odds. Helen took to the stage, with Anne Sullivan by her side to assist with communication. The audience fell silent as Helen began to speak, her clear and measured words captivating everyone in the room.

Helen talked about her early childhood, the illness that had left her blind and deaf, and the breakthrough moment at the water pump. She described her education journey, emphasizing the critical role that Anne Sullivan had played in her life. Helen's words were filled with gratitude, hope, and a call to action. She urged the audience to support initiatives that provided education and opportunities for people with disabilities.

Helen's speeches were not just about sharing her story; they were also about advocating for change. She spoke passionately about the need for inclusive education, better job opportunities, and greater social acceptance for people with disabilities. Helen used her platform to challenge societal prejudices and push for policies that would improve the lives of those who, like her, faced significant barriers.

As Helen's reputation as a public speaker grew, she traveled extensively, both within the United States and internationally. She gave speeches in major cities around the world, from London to Tokyo, each time drawing large crowds and media attention. Helen's ability to communicate across cultures and languages made her a global ambassador for disability rights.

During her travels, Helen met with political leaders, educators, and activists. She used these opportunities to advocate for policy changes and increased funding for programs that supported people with disabilities. Helen's influence was instrumental in the establishment of many initiatives that improved accessibility and inclusion in education and the workplace.

One of the challenges Helen faced as a public speaker was the physical and mental toll of constant travel and speaking engagements. The demands of her schedule were exhausting, and there were times when she felt overwhelmed by the pressures of her work. Yet, Helen's commitment to her cause kept her going. She believed deeply in the power of her message and the impact she could have on the world.

Helen's speeches often included anecdotes and stories that made her message relatable and engaging. She would share humorous or poignant moments from her life, illustrating her points with vivid descriptions. These personal touches made her speeches not only informative but also deeply moving. Audiences left feeling inspired and motivated to take action.

One of Helen's favorite stories to share was about her first visit to the zoo as a child. She described how she had felt the rough skin of an elephant, the smooth scales of a snake, and the soft fur of a rabbit. These tactile experiences had given her a sense of the diversity of the animal kingdom, even though she couldn't see or hear the animals. This story highlighted the importance of accessibility and the ways in which people with disabilities could experience and enjoy the world around them.

In addition to her public speaking, Helen wrote extensively, authoring numerous articles and books that further spread her message. Her writing complemented her speeches, allowing her to reach an even wider audience. Helen's autobiography,

"The Story of My Life," became a bestseller and was translated into multiple languages, bringing her story to readers around the globe.

Helen's work as a public speaker was not limited to disability rights. She also spoke about broader social issues, including women's suffrage, labor rights, and pacifism. Helen was a passionate advocate for social justice, believing that everyone deserved equal opportunities and respect. Her speeches often addressed the interconnectedness of various social causes, urging people to work together to create a more equitable and compassionate world.

advocacy for people with disabilities

One of the central pillars of Helen's advocacy was education. Having benefited immensely from her own education, Helen was a staunch believer in the power of knowledge to transform lives. She campaigned tirelessly for accessible education for all, emphasizing that children with disabilities had the right to the same educational opportunities as their peers. Helen's speeches and writings highlighted the importance of specialized teaching methods, proper training for educators, and the need for schools to be equipped with resources like Braille books and assistive technologies.

Helen often spoke about her own experiences to illustrate the potential within every child, no matter their disabilities. She recounted how Anne Sullivan had opened up the world for her through innovative and patient teaching. Helen's story served as a powerful testament to what could be achieved with the right support. She argued that investing in education for children with disabilities was not just an act of charity but a wise investment in the future, as these children could grow up to be valuable, contributing members of society.

In addition to education, Helen focused on improving employment opportunities for people with disabilities. She believed that everyone should have the chance to work and contribute to their community. Helen advocated for inclusive hiring practices and workplace accommodations that would allow people with disabilities to perform their jobs effectively. She worked with organizations and businesses to promote the idea that employing people with disabilities was not only the right thing to do but also beneficial for the economy.

Helen's advocacy extended to healthcare as well. She campaigned for better medical care and services for people with disabilities, recognizing that many faced significant barriers to accessing the healthcare they needed. She pushed for policies that would provide comprehensive medical support, including routine check-ups, physical therapy, and mental health services. Helen's efforts helped to raise awareness about the unique healthcare needs of people with disabilities and the importance of addressing these needs to improve their quality of life.

Throughout her advocacy work, Helen collaborated with numerous organizations dedicated to supporting people with disabilities. One of the most notable was the American Foundation for the Blind (AFB), with which she had a long and impactful association. Helen worked with the AFB to promote Braille literacy, increase funding for services for the blind, and advocate for legislation that would protect the rights of people with disabilities. Her involvement with the AFB helped to amplify her message and bring about tangible changes in policies and public attitudes.

Helen's advocacy was not limited to the United States. She traveled extensively, meeting with leaders and activists from around the world to discuss disability rights and share best practices. Her international work helped to build a global network of advocates committed to improving the lives of people with disabilities. Helen's visits to countries like Japan, South Africa, and India were met with widespread acclaim, and she often returned from these trips with new insights and renewed determination.

One of the key aspects of Helen's advocacy was her ability to connect with people on a personal level. She had a unique gift for making complex issues relatable and understandable. Helen's speeches and writings were filled with personal anecdotes and vivid descriptions that made her audience feel the weight of her message. She could convey the daily struggles and triumphs of living with a disability in a way that resonated deeply with both policymakers and the general public.

Helen's advocacy was also characterized by her unyielding optimism. She believed in the potential for change and the goodness of people. This optimism was infectious and inspired many to join her cause. Helen's positive outlook and unwavering belief in the power of advocacy to bring about social justice were crucial in mobilizing support and driving forward her agenda.

One memorable example of Helen's impact was her role in the passage of the Wagner-O'Day Act in 1938. This legislation required the federal government to purchase certain products made by blind workers, thereby creating employment opportunities and supporting industries that employed people with disabilities. Helen's testimony before Congress was instrumental in garnering support for the bill. She spoke passionately about the need to provide meaningful work for blind individuals and the dignity that comes with employment. The passage of the Wagner-O'Day Act was a significant victory and a testament to Helen's persuasive advocacy.

Helen Keller's advocacy work was not without its challenges. She often faced resistance from those who believed that people with disabilities should be segregated and not integrated into mainstream society. There were also times when her own disabilities made it difficult to communicate her message. However, Helen's determination never wavered. She used every tool at her disposal, from her writing to her public speaking, to continue fighting for the rights of people with disabilities.

One of Helen's most profound statements about her advocacy came during a speech she gave late in her life. She said, "Alone we can do so little; together we can do so much." This sentiment encapsulated her belief in the power of collective action and the importance of community in driving social change. Helen's work was always about bringing people together to achieve a common goal – a world where everyone, regardless of their abilities, could live with dignity and opportunity.

involvement in social and political causes

One of Helen's earliest and most enduring commitments was to the women's suffrage movement. Growing up in a time when women did not have the right to vote, Helen was acutely aware of the injustices faced by women. She believed passionately that women should have the same political rights as men, including the right to vote and participate fully in democratic processes. Helen joined forces with prominent suffragists, attending rallies and speaking at events to advocate for women's suffrage.

Helen's speeches on women's rights were powerful and compelling. She often drew parallels between the struggles of women and those of people with disabilities, emphasizing the need for equality and inclusion in all aspects of society. Her eloquence and conviction helped to galvanize support for the suffrage movement, and she celebrated alongside other suffragists when women finally won the right to vote in 1920 with the ratification of the 19th Amendment.

In addition to her work for women's rights, Helen was a vocal advocate for labor rights. She was deeply concerned about the exploitation of workers and the harsh conditions many faced, particularly in industrial settings. Helen supported the labor movement and championed the rights of workers to fair wages, reasonable working hours, and safe working conditions. She believed that economic justice was essential to social justice and that the well-being of workers was fundamental to a healthy society.

Helen's involvement with the labor movement brought her into contact with various labor leaders and organizations. She marched in labor parades, spoke at union meetings, and used her platform to highlight the plight of workers. Helen's advocacy for labor rights was rooted in her belief that all individuals deserved dignity and respect, regardless of their social or economic status.

Another significant aspect of Helen's social activism was her commitment to pacifism and anti-war efforts. Having lived through both World War I and World War II, Helen was deeply troubled by the devastation and loss caused by war. She believed that war was a senseless and destructive force that only served to perpetuate suffering and injustice. Helen became an outspoken critic of militarism and advocated for peaceful solutions to conflicts.

Helen's pacifist stance was influenced by her association with the American Civil Liberties Union (ACLU) and other peace organizations. She wrote extensively about the horrors of war and the importance of diplomacy and international cooperation. Helen's anti-war activism was not always popular, especially during times of heightened nationalism and conflict, but she remained steadfast in her commitment to peace.

Helen's social and political activism also extended to issues of racial equality. She was a strong supporter of the civil rights movement and believed that racial discrimination was a grave injustice that needed to be eradicated. Helen spoke out against segregation and racial violence, calling for equality and justice for African Americans. She admired and supported leaders like W.E.B. Du Bois and later, Martin Luther King Jr., and her advocacy helped to bring attention to the struggles for racial equality.

Helen's dedication to social justice was evident in her support for various progressive causes. She was an advocate for birth control and reproductive rights, believing that women should have the autonomy to make decisions about their own bodies. Helen also supported the emerging environmental movement, recognizing the importance of protecting natural resources and promoting sustainable practices.

Throughout her life, Helen's activism was characterized by a deep empathy for those who were marginalized and oppressed. She used her platform to amplify the voices of those who were often unheard and to call for systemic changes that would create a more just and equitable society. Helen's intersectional approach to activism—addressing issues of disability, gender, labor, race, and peace—demonstrated her holistic understanding of social justice.

Helen Keller's involvement in social and political causes was not without its challenges. Her outspoken views sometimes attracted criticism and controversy. There were moments when her advocacy put her at odds with powerful interests and prevailing public opinions. However, Helen was undeterred by opposition. She believed that speaking out against injustice was a moral imperative, even when it was difficult or unpopular.

One of the most remarkable aspects of Helen's activism was her ability to connect with diverse audiences. She was able to engage with people from different backgrounds and perspectives, building coalitions and fostering dialogue. Helen's approach to activism was inclusive and collaborative, recognizing that meaningful change required the efforts of many.

6 / writing and achievements

helen's books and publications

HELEN KELLER WAS NOT ONLY a remarkable advocate and speaker but also a prolific writer whose books and publications left an indelible mark on literature and social advocacy. Her writings provided a window into her world and offered profound insights into her thoughts, experiences, and unwavering determination to make a difference. Helen's ability to articulate her ideas and emotions so beautifully made her an influential author whose works continue to inspire readers around the globe.

Helen's most famous work, "The Story of My Life," was published in 1903 when she was just 23 years old. This autobiography chronicles her early years, the illness that left her blind and deaf, and the transformative journey she undertook with the help of her teacher, Anne Sullivan. The book's vivid descriptions and heartfelt narrative captivated readers, providing a deep understanding of Helen's challenges and triumphs. "The Story of My Life" became an instant bestseller and was translated into multiple languages, bringing Helen's story to an international audience.

One of the most striking aspects of "The Story of My Life" is Helen's eloquent and evocative writing style. She described her experiences with a clarity and emotional depth that resonated with readers. The book not only highlighted her personal journey but also underscored the importance of education, perseverance, and the human spirit's resilience. Helen's ability to convey complex emotions and sensory experiences, despite her disabilities, showcased her extraordinary talent as a writer.

Following the success of her autobiography, Helen continued to write extensively. Her second book, "Optimism: An Essay," published in 1903, delved into her philosophy of life. In this work, Helen explored the concept of optimism, arguing that a positive outlook and a belief in the inherent goodness of people could help overcome adversity. She drew on her own experiences to illustrate how optimism had played a crucial role in her life, enabling her to face challenges with courage and determination.

Helen's essay on optimism was more than just a personal reflection; it was a call to action. She encouraged readers to adopt an optimistic mindset and to work towards creating a better world. Helen's belief in the power of positive thinking and her conviction that each individual could make a difference were central themes in her advocacy work and writings.

In 1910, Helen published "The World I Live In," a collection of essays that provided further insight into her inner world. The essays covered a range of topics, from her daily life and sensory experiences to her thoughts on literature and philosophy. Through these essays, Helen invited readers to see the world through her perspective, offering a unique and intimate glimpse into her mind.

"The World I Live In" was praised for its poetic language and profound observations. Helen's ability to describe her sensory experiences, despite her blindness and deafness, was nothing short of remarkable. She conveyed the textures, shapes, and emotions of her world with a richness and precision that left readers in awe. This book further cemented Helen's reputation as a gifted writer and thinker.

Helen's literary contributions extended beyond personal reflections and philosophy. She was also a keen social commentator, using her writings to advocate for social justice and equality. In 1913, she published "Out of the Dark: Essays, Letters, and Addresses on Physical and Social Vision." This collection of essays and speeches addressed a wide range of social issues, including disability rights, women's suffrage, labor rights, and pacifism.

"Out of the Dark" showcased Helen's deep commitment to social advocacy and her ability to engage with complex social and political issues. Her writings were passionate and persuasive, calling for systemic changes to address the injustices faced by marginalized communities. Helen's essays reflected her belief that true progress could only be achieved through empathy, education, and collective action.

Throughout her life, Helen continued to write on various subjects, contributing articles to newspapers and magazines. Her writings covered a diverse array of topics, from education and disability rights to literature and personal reflections. Each piece she wrote carried her distinct voice and her unwavering commitment to making the world a better place.

Helen's literary legacy also includes several books for young readers. She understood the importance of reaching out to children and inspiring them with stories of resilience and courage. One such book, "The Story of My Life for Young Readers," adapted her autobiography for a younger audience. Helen hoped that her story would encourage children to persevere in the face of challenges and to believe in their own potential.

In addition to her own books, Helen was an avid reader and admirer of other authors. She often referenced her favorite writers in her works, drawing inspiration from their ideas and story-telling techniques. Helen's love for literature was evident in her extensive reading list, which included classics by authors such as Shakespeare, Dickens, and Twain. Her deep appreciation for the written word enriched her own writing and informed her advocacy work.

Helen Keller's books and publications were more than just literary achievements; they were powerful tools for social change. Through her writings, Helen educated the public about the experiences of people with disabilities, challenged societal prejudices, and advocated for greater inclusivity and equality. Her ability to connect with readers on an emotional and intellectual level made her a compelling and influential voice in the fight for social justice.

awards and recognitions

Throughout her remarkable life, Helen Keller received numerous awards and recognitions that honored her contributions to literature, advocacy, and social justice. Each award and recognition reflected the profound impact she had on the world and the enduring legacy of her work. These accolades were not just a testament to Helen's achievements, but also a celebration of her spirit, determination, and unwavering commitment to making the world a better place.

One of the earliest and most significant recognitions Helen received was the honorary degree of Doctor of Humane Letters from Harvard University in 1955. This prestigious award was a historic moment, as Helen became the first deaf-blind person to receive an honorary degree from Harvard. The degree recognized her outstanding contributions to literature and her tireless advocacy for people with disabilities. The ceremony was a proud moment for Helen, Anne Sullivan, and their many supporters who had witnessed her incredible journey.

Another major milestone in Helen's life was being awarded the Presidential Medal of Freedom in 1964 by President Lyndon B. Johnson. The Presidential Medal of Freedom is one of the highest civilian honors in the United States, awarded to individuals who have made significant contributions to the security or national interests of the country, world peace, or cultural or other significant public or private endeavors. Helen was deeply moved by this recognition, which celebrated her lifelong dedication to advocating for the rights and dignity of people with disabilities, as well as her broader contributions to social justice.

Helen's international influence was also recognized through various awards and honors from countries around the world. She received the Chevalier of the French Legion of Honor in 1952, one of France's highest decorations. This honor was a reflection of Helen's impact on a global scale and her efforts to promote understanding and cooperation between nations. The award celebrated her work in advancing the rights of people with disabilities and her contributions to international peace and goodwill.

In addition to these major awards, Helen

received numerous accolades from organizations dedicated to social justice, education, and disability rights. The American Foundation for the Blind (AFB), with which Helen had a long and impactful association, awarded her the Migel Medal in 1932. The Migel Medal is the highest honor given by the AFB, recognizing individuals who have made extraordinary contributions to improving the lives of people who are blind or visually impaired. Helen's work with the AFB had transformed countless lives, and this award was a fitting tribute to her tireless efforts.

Helen's influence extended to the academic world, where she was awarded honorary degrees from numerous universities, including Temple University, the University of Glasgow, and the University of Delhi. These honorary degrees celebrated her intellectual contributions and her role as a trailblazer in education and advocacy for people with disabilities. Each degree was a recognition of Helen's profound impact on academia and her commitment to promoting knowledge and understanding.

In 1956, Helen was honored with the Eleanor Roosevelt Humanitarian Award. Named after the former First Lady and a fellow advocate for human rights, this award recognized Helen's unwavering dedication to improving the lives of others. Eleanor Roosevelt and Helen Keller shared a deep friendship and mutual respect, both women having dedicated their lives to social justice and humanitarian causes. This award was particularly meaningful for Helen, as it honored her legacy alongside that of a dear friend and fellow champion of equality.

Helen's literary contributions were also celebrated with various awards and recognitions. Her autobiography, "The Story of My Life," continued to be recognized as a literary classic, inspiring generations of readers. The book received numerous accolades for its eloquence, emotional depth, and powerful storytelling. Helen's ability to convey her experiences with such clarity and grace left a lasting impression on readers and critics alike.

The global recognition of Helen's work was further evidenced by the numerous streets, schools, and institutions named in her honor. These dedications were a testament to the widespread admiration and respect for Helen's contributions. The Helen Keller International organization, founded in her honor, continues to carry forward her legacy by combating the causes and consequences of blindness and malnutrition worldwide. This organization's work is a living tribute to Helen's vision and commitment to making a difference in the lives of those in need.

In addition to formal awards and recognitions, Helen received countless letters, accolades, and tributes from individuals and organizations around the world. People from all walks of life were inspired by her story and her advocacy. These personal tributes were a source of great joy and motivation for Helen, reminding her of the far-reaching impact of her work.

Helen Keller's awards and recognitions were not just acknowledgments of her achievements; they were symbols of the barriers she had broken and the lives she had touched. Each accolade reflected a chapter in her journey, a journey marked by perseverance, courage, and an unwavering belief in the power of education and advocacy to create change.

influence on future generations

One of the most profound ways Helen has influenced future generations is through her work in promoting education for people with disabilities. Her advocacy helped to break down barriers and create opportunities for individuals who were previously marginalized and overlooked. Schools and educational programs around the world have been inspired by Helen's story, leading to more inclusive and accessible learning environments. Her belief that every child, regardless of their abilities, deserves the right to a quality education has become a guiding principle for educators and policymakers.

Helen's impact on education is evident in the numerous institutions named in her honor. Schools, libraries, and educational programs bearing her name continue to embody her values and commitment to inclusivity. These institutions serve as living tributes to Helen's legacy, fostering environments where students with disabilities can thrive and reach their full potential. Helen Keller International, an organization founded in her honor, continues to work globally to combat blindness and malnutrition, further extending her influence on health and education.

Helen's story has also been a source of inspiration for countless individuals pursuing careers in special education, rehabilitation, and disability advocacy. Her example has motivated many to dedicate their lives to supporting and empowering people with disabilities. These professionals often cite Helen's life as a catalyst for their own journeys, demonstrating the profound ripple effect of her advocacy and achievements.

In addition to her contributions to education, Helen Keller's influence is deeply felt in the realm of social justice and human rights. Her tireless work to promote equality and dignity for all people, regardless of their abilities, has inspired generations of activists and advocates. Helen's intersectional approach to advocacy—addressing issues of disability, gender, labor rights, and racial equality—has become a model for modern social justice movements.

Helen's writings and speeches continue to resonate with those fighting for social change. Her words, filled with empathy, insight, and unwavering resolve, have been quoted and referenced by activists, leaders, and educators worldwide. Helen's ability to articulate the struggles and triumphs of marginalized communities has provided a powerful voice for those who often go unheard. Her advocacy for peace, equality, and justice remains a cornerstone of human rights discourse.

The arts and literature have also been profoundly influenced by Helen Keller's life and work. Her autobiography, "The Story of My Life," and other writings have inspired numerous adaptations, including films, plays, and books. These adaptations bring Helen's story to new audiences, ensuring that her legacy continues to inspire creativity and storytelling. The Broadway play and subsequent film "The Miracle Worker," which dramatizes Helen's early years and her relationship with Anne Sullivan, have become iconic representations of her journey and the power of perseverance.

Helen's influence extends to popular culture, where her story is often referenced as a symbol of overcoming adversity. She is frequently cited in motivational speeches, self-help books, and inspirational quotes, serving as a timeless example of resilience and determination. Helen's ability to rise above her challenges and make a significant impact on the world continues to motivate people to pursue their dreams and make a difference, regardless of the obstacles they face.

In the field of disability rights, Helen Keller's legacy is particularly profound. Her advocacy laid the groundwork for many of the advances in accessibility and inclusion that we see today. Laws such as the Americans with Disabilities Act (ADA) and the Individuals with Disabilities Education Act (IDEA) were influenced by the principles Helen championed throughout her life. These laws have transformed the landscape for people with disabilities, ensuring greater access to education, employment, and public services.

Helen's legacy also lives on through the countless individuals who draw inspiration from her story to advocate for change in their own communities. Her example has empowered people with disabilities to speak out, demand their rights, and challenge societal prejudices. Helen's life demonstrates that advocacy and activism can drive significant social change, and her story continues to inspire new generations of leaders in the disability rights movement.

Helen Keller's influence is also evident in the global community, where her advocacy has inspired international efforts to improve the lives of people with disabilities. Organizations and governments worldwide have adopted her principles, working to create more inclusive societies. Helen's vision of a world where everyone, regardless of their abilities, can live with dignity and opportunity has become a global aspiration.

7 / friendship and support

relationship with anne sullivan

WHEN ANNE SULLIVAN arrived at the Keller household in 1887, Helen was a nearly seven-year-old child trapped in a world of silence and darkness. She was frustrated and isolated, unable to communicate her thoughts and feelings. Anne, who had herself endured significant hardships, including partial blindness, understood the importance of empathy and patience in teaching Helen. From the moment they met, Anne approached Helen with a blend of firmness and compassion, laying the groundwork for a transformative relationship.

One of the most famous moments in their relationship occurred shortly after Anne's arrival. The breakthrough at the water pump, where Helen first connected the feeling of water with the spelled word "w-a-t-e-r," was a pivotal moment. This breakthrough was not just a victory in communication but also the beginning of a deep bond between teacher and student. Anne's innovative teaching methods and persistence unlocked Helen's potential, opening a world of learning and possibilities.

Anne's role extended far beyond that of a traditional teacher. She became Helen's interpreter, guide, and constant companion. Their days were filled with lessons that covered a wide range of subjects, from language and mathematics to history and geography. Anne tailored her teaching methods to Helen's unique needs, using tactile and experiential learning techniques. This personalized approach allowed Helen to grasp complex concepts and fostered a love of learning that would stay with her throughout her life.

The relationship between Helen and Anne was characterized by intense dedication and tireless effort. Anne's teaching methods were often demanding, requiring Helen to push her limits and persevere through frustration. Despite the challenges, Helen thrived under Anne's guidance, developing a deep sense of discipline and resilience. The trust and respect that grew between them were essential to Helen's educational success.

As Helen's abilities and confidence grew, their relationship evolved. They became partners in advocacy, working together to promote education and rights for people with disabilities. Anne's influence was evident in Helen's public speaking and writing, where she often spoke of the transformative power of education and the importance of support and mentorship. Their partnership demonstrated that with the right guidance, individuals with disabilities could achieve great things.

Anne's commitment to Helen extended to her personal life as well. She provided emotional support and encouragement, helping Helen navigate the complexities of social interactions and personal relationships. Anne's unwavering belief in Helen's potential helped her overcome self-doubt and societal prejudices. This support was crucial as Helen faced the challenges of higher education, public speaking, and advocacy work.

The bond between Helen and Anne was tested by various challenges, including Anne's declining health. Anne suffered from multiple health issues throughout her life, which sometimes affected her ability to assist Helen. Despite these difficulties, Anne remained dedicated to Helen's success. Their relationship was a testament to the power of perseverance and the deep connection that can develop between a teacher and student.

As Helen grew older and more independent, their relationship continued to evolve. Anne remained a central figure in Helen's life, providing guidance and support even as Helen became a renowned author and advocate. Their partnership exemplified the enduring impact of a positive mentor-student relationship, demonstrating how such a bond can shape an individual's life and legacy.

One of the most touching aspects of their relationship was the mutual admiration and gratitude they expressed for each other. Helen often spoke of Anne with profound respect and affection, crediting her with opening the doors to the world of knowledge and communication. Anne, in turn, was immensely proud of Helen's achievements and the barriers she had overcome. Their relationship was built on a foundation of love and mutual respect, which remained strong until Anne's death in 1936.

After Anne's passing, Helen continued to honor her memory through her work and advocacy. She often reflected on the lessons Anne had taught her and the impact she had on her life. Helen's continued success and influence were a living tribute to the partnership they had shared. The principles of dedication, resilience, and the transformative power of education that Anne instilled in Helen continued to guide her throughout her life.

Helen and Anne's relationship has been immortalized in numerous books, plays, and films, most notably in the play and film "The Miracle Worker." These portrayals capture the essence of their bond and the incredible journey they undertook together. Their story continues to inspire educators, students, and advocates, highlighting the importance of mentorship, patience, and belief in the potential of every individual.

other important figures in helen's life

Kate Keller, Helen's mother was instrumental in seeking help for Helen after she lost her sight and hearing. Her relentless pursuit of resources and support led to the life-changing arrival of Anne Sullivan. Kate's dedication and love provided a foundation of stability and encouragement, enabling Helen to thrive. Kate remained a steadfast supporter of Helen's education and advocacy work, offering emotional and practical support throughout her life.

Helen's father, Arthur Keller, also played a significant role in her early years. Although initially skeptical about the effectiveness of formal education for Helen, he eventually embraced Anne Sullivan's efforts and supported Helen's educational journey. Arthur's support extended to ensuring that Helen had the resources and opportunities she needed to succeed. His acceptance and backing were crucial in facilitating the environment in which Helen could flourish.

Another important figure was Alexander Graham Bell, the famous inventor and educator. Bell's work with the deaf community brought him into contact with the Keller family, and he played a pivotal role in connecting them with the Perkins Institute for the Blind, where Anne Sullivan was educated. Bell's belief in the potential of individuals with disabilities and his advocacy for their education and integration into society resonated deeply with Helen. His influence extended beyond their initial meeting, as he remained a lifelong friend and mentor to Helen.

Michael Anagnos, the director of the Perkins Institute for the Blind, was also instrumental in Helen's life. He supported Anne Sullivan's mission to educate Helen and provided the resources and encouragement needed for her early education.

Anagnos recognized Helen's extraordinary potential and facilitated opportunities for her to learn and grow. His support and belief in Helen's abilities were critical during the formative years of her education.

John Macy, a writer and literary critic, played a significant role in Helen's literary career. He was married to Anne Sullivan and became an important collaborator in Helen's writing endeavors. John helped Helen refine her writing skills and navigate the complexities of publishing. His literary insights and editorial guidance were invaluable in the creation of Helen's works, including her famous autobiography, "The Story of My Life." John's contributions extended beyond professional support, as he also provided personal encouragement and friendship.

Helen's relationship with Polly Thomson, another dedicated companion, was equally significant. After Anne Sullivan's health began to decline, Polly Thomson took on the role of Helen's aide and interpreter. Polly's support was crucial in maintaining the continuity of Helen's work and daily life. She traveled with Helen, assisting her in her public speaking engagements and daily activities. Polly's dedication and care provided a sense of security and stability, allowing Helen to continue her advocacy and educational efforts despite the challenges posed by Anne's declining health.

One of Helen's dearest friends was Mark Twain, the renowned author. Twain admired Helen's courage and intellect, and their friendship blossomed over shared interests and mutual respect. Twain's wit and wisdom provided Helen with companionship and intellectual stimulation. He often praised Helen publicly, highlighting her achievements and advocating for her causes. Their friendship was a source of joy and inspiration for Helen, and Twain's support helped raise awareness of her work and the issues she championed.

Helen's interactions with Franklin D. Roosevelt and Eleanor Roosevelt further exemplified the important connections she made throughout her life. The Roosevelts admired Helen's advocacy work and supported her efforts to improve the lives of people with disabilities. Eleanor Roosevelt, in particular, shared Helen's passion for social justice and human rights. Their friendship was based on mutual respect and a shared commitment to creating a more equitable society.

Helen also formed significant relationships with various political leaders, educators, and activists around the world. Her international travels introduced her to numerous influential figures who supported her advocacy work. These connections helped Helen expand her reach and impact, enabling her to promote disability rights and education on a global scale.

Throughout her life, Helen's network of supporters and friends played crucial roles in her personal and professional development. Each relationship brought unique contributions, enriching Helen's experiences and providing the support she needed to overcome challenges and achieve her goals. The collective impact of these individuals demonstrates the importance of community and collaboration in driving social change and personal growth.

community and network of supporters

The foundation of Helen's network of supporters was built during her early years, particularly through the connections made by her parents and Anne Sullivan. One of the earliest and most influential supporters was Alexander Graham Bell. Renowned for his invention of the telephone, Bell was also a passionate advocate for the deaf community. He met Helen when she was just a child and played a pivotal role in connecting the

Keller family with the Perkins Institute for the Blind. Bell's belief in Helen's potential and his continued support throughout her life were instrumental in her development.

The Perkins Institute itself became a cornerstone of Helen's support network. Under the guidance of Michael Anagnos, the Institute provided Helen with educational resources and connected her with Anne Sullivan. The teachers and staff at Perkins were deeply invested in Helen's success, offering her opportunities to learn and grow in ways that were previously unimaginable. The relationships Helen formed at Perkins, both with educators and fellow students, were vital in shaping her early experiences and instilling in her a love of learning.

As Helen's fame and influence grew, so did her network of supporters. Among these was John Macy, who, along with his wife Anne Sullivan, played a crucial role in Helen's literary career. John's editorial guidance and support helped Helen navigate the complexities of writing and publishing. His belief in her abilities and his commitment to her success were invaluable as Helen embarked on her journey as an author.

Helen's friendship with Mark Twain was another significant relationship that provided both personal and professional support. Twain's admiration for Helen's courage and intellect was evident in his public endorsements and private correspondences. He often used his platform to highlight Helen's achievements and advocate for her causes. Twain's wit and wisdom offered Helen a unique form of companionship and intellectual stimulation, enriching her life and work.

In addition to these personal relationships, Helen's involvement with various organizations expanded her network and provided essential support for her advocacy efforts. The American Foundation for the Blind (AFB) was one such organization that played a crucial role in Helen's life. Helen worked closely with the AFB to promote Braille literacy, improve educational opportunities for the blind, and advocate for policies that supported people with visual impairments. The AFB's resources and platforms enabled Helen to reach a broader audience and effect significant change.

Helen's network also included numerous political figures who supported her advocacy work. Franklin D. Roosevelt and Eleanor Roosevelt were among the most notable. Their admiration for Helen's dedication to social justice and disability rights fostered a mutual respect and collaboration. Eleanor Roosevelt, in particular, shared Helen's passion for human rights and frequently supported her initiatives. Their relationship highlighted the power of alliances in advancing social causes and creating lasting change.

Internationally, Helen's travels introduced her to a diverse array of supporters who shared her vision for a more inclusive world. Leaders and activists from various countries admired Helen's resilience and were inspired by her advocacy. These global connections helped Helen expand her influence beyond the United States, allowing her to promote disability rights on an international stage. Her work with organizations such as the League of Nations further exemplified her commitment to global advocacy.

Helen's network was not limited to high-profile figures; it also included countless individuals who were inspired by her story and dedicated to supporting her mission. These supporters ranged from educators and healthcare professionals to fellow advocates and everyday citizens. Their collective efforts helped sustain Helen's work and amplify her message. Community events, fundraising efforts, and grassroots campaigns organized by these supporters were crucial in advancing Helen's advocacy and raising awareness about disability rights.

The sense of community and shared purpose among Helen's supporters was a source of strength and motivation for her. Their belief in her mission and their willingness to stand by her through challenges reinforced Helen's determination to continue her work. This network of support was essential in navigating the complexities of advocacy and ensuring that Helen's message reached those who needed it most.

Helen's relationship with her supporters was reciprocal; she inspired and empowered them just as they supported her. Her ability to connect with people on a personal level, share her story, and articulate her vision for a more inclusive world resonated deeply with her supporters. Helen's speeches, writings, and public appearances were not only calls to action but also expressions of gratitude and solidarity with those who stood by her.

One of the most remarkable aspects of Helen's network was its diversity. It included people from various backgrounds, professions, and walks of life, united by a common goal of promoting equality and justice. This diversity enriched Helen's perspective and broadened the scope of her advocacy. It also demonstrated the universal appeal of her message and the widespread recognition of the importance of disability rights.

8 / legacy and inspiration

HELEN KELLER'S remarkable life and achievements have left an enduring impact on society, transcending her own personal story to inspire generations and drive significant social change. Her legacy is multifaceted, touching on education, disability rights, advocacy, literature, and social justice. Helen's contributions continue to resonate today, shaping how we think about inclusivity, accessibility, and the potential of the human spirit.

Helen's advocacy for disability rights laid the groundwork for many of the advances we see today. She was a tireless advocate for Braille literacy, accessible education, and employment opportunities for people with disabilities. Her work with organizations like the American Foundation for the Blind (AFB) helped to improve the lives of countless individuals by advocating for policies that promoted equality and accessibility. The principles Helen championed continue to inform contemporary disability rights movements and legislative efforts.

One of the most tangible legacies of Helen Keller's impact is the Americans with Disabilities Act (ADA), passed in 1990. While Helen did not live to see its enactment, her advocacy and the awareness she raised about the rights and capabilities of people with disabilities were instrumental in shaping the cultural and political climate that made such legislation possible. The ADA has transformed the landscape for individuals with disabilities in the United States, ensuring greater access to education, employment, public services, and accommodations.

Helen's influence extended beyond the realm of disability rights into broader social justice issues. She was a vocal advocate for women's suffrage, labor rights, and racial equality. Her intersectional approach to advocacy highlighted the interconnectedness of various social causes, a perspective that remains relevant and influential in contemporary social justice movements. Helen's commitment to fighting for a more equitable and just society continues to inspire activists and advocates across the globe.

Education was another area where Helen's impact was profound. Her own educational journey, guided by Anne Sullivan, showcased the transformative power of learning and the importance of accessible education. Helen's story has inspired countless educators to develop innovative teaching methods and create inclusive learning environments. Schools and educational programs worldwide continue to draw inspiration from Helen's life, emphasizing the potential within every student, regardless of their abilities.

Helen's literary contributions have also left a lasting mark. Her autobiography, "The Story of My Life," remains a classic, inspiring readers with its eloquence and emotional depth. Helen's ability to convey her experiences and insights through writing has touched millions of lives. Her other works, including essays and speeches, continue to be studied and admired for their clarity, passion, and advocacy for social change. Helen's writings provide a valuable perspective on the challenges and triumphs of living with a disability and the broader fight for human rights.

Helen's influence is also evident in the numerous honors and recognitions she received throughout her life. From the Presidential Medal of Freedom to honorary degrees from prestigious universities, these accolades reflect the widespread admiration for her contributions to society. Institutions named in her honor, such as schools, libraries, and organizations, serve as ongoing reminders of her legacy and the impact of her work.

The Helen Keller International organization, founded in her honor, continues her mission by addressing causes of blindness and malnutrition worldwide. This organization embodies Helen's commitment to improving the lives of the most vulnerable and demonstrates the enduring relevance of her vision for a more equitable world. The work of Helen Keller International has helped millions of people, ensuring that Helen's legacy of compassion and advocacy lives on.

Helen Keller's story has been immortalized in various cultural forms, including books, plays, and films. "The Miracle Worker," both as a play and a film, dramatizes Helen's early years and her relationship with Anne Sullivan, bringing her story to new audiences and highlighting the power of perseverance and education. These portrayals continue to inspire and educate, keeping Helen's legacy alive for future generations.

Helen's impact is also felt on a personal level by

individuals who draw inspiration from her life. Her story has motivated countless people to overcome their own challenges and pursue their dreams. Helen's resilience, determination, and unwavering belief in the potential of every individual serve as a powerful source of inspiration. Her life demonstrates that with the right support and determination, seemingly insurmountable obstacles can be overcome.

As society continues to evolve, Helen Keller's legacy remains a guiding light for efforts to create a more inclusive and equitable world. Her life's work serves as a reminder of the importance of empathy, education, and advocacy. Helen's influence extends across generations, inspiring individuals and communities to strive for justice and equality.

Reflecting on Helen Keller's lasting impact, we see a legacy that transcends time and place. Her contributions have shaped societal attitudes, informed policy changes, and inspired countless individuals to pursue advocacy and social justice. Helen's story is a testament to the transformative power of education, the importance of resilience, and the potential within each of us to make a difference.

Helen Keller’s life continues to inspire and motivate, reminding us of the profound impact one person can have on the world. Her legacy is a call to action, encouraging us to work towards a future where everyone, regardless of their abilities, can achieve their full potential and live with dignity and respect. As we honor Helen Keller's contributions, we are reminded of the enduring power of the human spirit and the importance of advocating for a more inclusive and just society.

fun facts

One intriguing aspect of Helen's life was her ability to enjoy music despite being deaf. Helen could sense the vibrations of music through her fingertips, an experience she described as deeply moving. She particularly enjoyed feeling the piano's vibrations and once said, "Music has always been a part of my life, and I have loved it passionately." This unique way of experiencing music highlights Helen's extraordinary ability to find joy and beauty in the world, even in unconventional ways.

Helen was also an accomplished author, having written 12 published books and numerous articles during her lifetime. Her first book, "The Story of My Life," published in 1903, remains one of the most famous autobiographies ever written. Helen's writing extended beyond her personal experiences;

she penned essays on a variety of topics, including politics, social issues, and even travel. Her literary talent and insightful perspectives earned her a place among the respected authors of her time.

In addition to her writing, Helen was a prolific traveler. Despite her disabilities, she traveled to 39 countries on five continents, advocating for the rights of people with disabilities and meeting with world leaders. Her travels were not only for advocacy; they also reflected her deep curiosity and desire to experience different cultures. Helen's international work helped to spread her message of inclusivity and education worldwide.

Helen Keller was also a dog lover. Throughout her life, she had several canine companions, each of whom brought her great joy and companionship. Her first dog, a Boston terrier named Phiz, was given to her by her friend and mentor, Alexander Graham Bell. Later in life, she had a beloved Akita named Kamikaze-Go, a gift from a Japanese police officer. Helen's love for her dogs was evident in her writings, where she often spoke about the comfort and companionship they provided her.

An interesting fact about Helen is her involvement in vaudeville. In the 1920s, Helen and Anne Sullivan performed on the vaudeville circuit to raise awareness and funds for the American Foundation for the Blind. Their act included a lecture on Helen's life and a question-and-answer session with the audience. This unconventional platform allowed Helen to reach a wide and diverse audience, showcasing her ability to adapt and find innovative ways to share her story and advocacy.

Helen's connection with prominent figures of her time extended beyond Alexander Graham Bell and Mark Twain. She was friends with many influential people, including Franklin D. Roosevelt, Charlie Chaplin, and Eleanor Roosevelt. These friendships were based on mutual respect and a shared commitment to social justice. Helen's ability to form meaningful connections with such diverse individuals speaks to her charisma and the universal appeal of her message.

Despite her busy schedule and public life, Helen found time for hobbies and interests. She enjoyed gardening and found great pleasure in tending to her flowers. Helen also loved to read, particularly enjoying works of classic literature. Shakespeare was one of her favorite authors, and she often referenced his plays and sonnets in her writings and speeches. Her love for literature was a constant source of inspiration and comfort throughout her life.

Helen's achievements in education were

groundbreaking. In addition to being the first deaf-blind person to earn a Bachelor of Arts degree from Radcliffe College, she also received honorary degrees from several prestigious universities, including Harvard, Temple University, and the University of Glasgow. These honors recognized her extraordinary accomplishments and her contributions to literature and social advocacy.

Another fascinating aspect of Helen's life was her involvement in politics. She was an active member of the Socialist Party and campaigned for various social reforms, including women's suffrage, labor rights, and pacifism. Helen's political activism was driven by her belief in equality and justice for all, and she used her platform to advocate for policies that aligned with these values. Her political engagement demonstrates her commitment to creating a more just and equitable society.

Helen's influence extended into the realm of science and technology. She was a close friend of Thomas Edison, who admired her resilience and intellect. Edison's invention of the phonograph provided Helen with a new way to experience the world of sound, further enhancing her understanding of music and spoken language. Helen's interactions with inventors and scientists of her time highlight her keen interest in technological advancements and their potential to improve the lives of people with disabilities.

One of the lesser-known but fascinating facts about Helen is her interest in and practice of spiritualism. She believed in the possibility of communication with the spirit world and attended seances with notable figures like Sir Arthur Conan Doyle. While this aspect of her life is less documented, it adds another layer to the complexity of Helen's character and her quest to understand the world beyond her immediate sensory experiences.

Helen Keller's story also intersects with significant historical events. She lived through both World War I and World War II, using these periods to advocate for peace and humanitarian efforts. Her work with organizations such as the American Civil Liberties Union (ACLU) and the Women's Peace Party reflected her commitment to pacifism and social justice. Helen's involvement in these movements demonstrated her unwavering dedication to creating a better world, even during times of global conflict.

In her later years, Helen continued to receive numerous accolades and honors for her work. In 1964, she was awarded the Presidential Medal of Freedom, one of the highest civilian honors in the United States. This award recognized her lifelong dedication to improving the lives of people with disabilities and her broader contributions to social justice. The numerous awards and recognitions Helen received throughout her life are a testament to her enduring impact and legacy.

conclusion

One of the most important lessons we can learn from Helen Keller is the power of perseverance. Helen faced immense challenges, but she never gave up. She kept pushing forward, even when things seemed impossible. This determination is something everyone can emulate. When kids encounter difficulties, whether it's in school, sports, or personal situations, remembering Helen's perseverance can help them stay motivated and focused.

Helen once said, "Optimism is the faith that leads to achievement. Nothing can be done without hope and confidence." This quote highlights the importance of maintaining a positive attitude. Optimism can be a powerful tool in overcoming challenges. When kids approach problems with hope and confidence, they are more likely to find solutions and keep going, even when the going gets tough.

Another key element in Helen's success was the support she received from those around her, particularly her teacher, Anne Sullivan. This support system played a crucial role in Helen's development and achievements. Kids should be encouraged to seek out support when they need it. Whether it's a teacher, a parent, a friend, or a coach, having someone to provide guidance, encouragement, and assistance can make a significant difference. It's important for kids to know that asking for help is a strength, not a weakness.

Helen's ability to communicate was a major breakthrough in her life. Learning to communicate opened up a world of possibilities for her. For kids, improving communication skills can help them express their needs, share their ideas, and connect with others. Encouraging kids to work on their communication skills, whether through speaking, writing, or using assistive technologies, can empower them to overcome barriers and achieve their goals.

Setting goals is another valuable strategy for overcoming challenges. Helen Keller achieved many of her accomplishments by setting clear, achievable goals and working tirelessly towards them. Kids can be encouraged to set their own goals, both big and small. These goals can provide direction and a sense of purpose. By breaking down larger goals into manageable steps, kids can make steady progress and celebrate their achievements along the way.

Resilience is a key theme in Helen Keller's life. She faced setbacks and disappointments but always found a way to bounce back and continue moving forward. Teaching kids about resilience can help them develop the ability to recover from difficulties. Resilience involves staying positive, adapting to change, and learning from mistakes. When kids understand that setbacks are a natural part of life, they can develop the strength to keep trying, even when things don't go as planned.

Helen's life also teaches us the importance of embracing our unique abilities and strengths. Despite her disabilities, Helen focused on what she could do rather than what she couldn't. Encouraging kids to recognize and develop their own strengths can boost their confidence and help them tackle challenges with a positive attitude. Whether they excel in art, sports, academics, or any other area, focusing on strengths can provide a solid foundation for overcoming obstacles.

One of the most inspiring aspects of Helen Keller's story is her ability to turn her challenges into opportunities. She didn't let her disabilities define her; instead, she used them as a platform to advocate for others and make a difference in the world. Kids can be encouraged to adopt a similar mindset. When faced with challenges, they can look for ways to learn and grow from the experience. Turning challenges into opportunities for growth and positive change can lead to personal development and a greater sense of accomplishment.

Empathy and kindness were central to Helen's advocacy work. She understood the struggles of others and dedicated her life to helping them. Encouraging kids to practice empathy and kindness can help them build strong relationships and create a supportive community. When kids understand and support each other, they can overcome challenges together. Acts of kindness, big or small, can make a significant impact and foster a positive environment.

Helen Keller's story is also a powerful reminder of the importance of education. Education was the key that unlocked the world for Helen, allowing her to achieve her dreams and make a lasting impact. Encouraging kids to value education and to see learning as a lifelong journey can empower them to overcome challenges. Education provides the tools and knowledge needed to navigate obstacles and seize opportunities.

Creative problem-solving is another valuable skill that can help kids overcome challenges. Helen and Anne Sullivan often had to think outside the box to find solutions to the unique challenges they faced. Encouraging kids to use their creativity and think critically can help them find innovative solutions to their own problems. Whether it's coming up with a new study method, finding a different approach to a task, or simply looking at a problem from a different perspective, creative problem-solving can be a powerful tool.

Helen Keller's achievements remind us that no dream is too big and no challenge is too great. Her life encourages us to dream big and work hard to achieve our goals. Kids should be encouraged to dream big and to believe in their ability to achieve those dreams. With determination, support, and a positive mindset, they can overcome any challenge and make their dreams a reality.

Helen once said, "The only thing worse than being blind is having sight but no vision." This powerful statement emphasizes the importance of having a vision for the future. Encouraging kids to think about their future and set long-term goals can help them stay focused and motivated. Having a vision provides direction and purpose, making it easier to overcome obstacles along the way.

glossary

1. Braille

Braille is a system of raised dots that can be felt with the fingertips. It is used by people who are blind or visually impaired to read and write. Each set of dots represents a letter, number, or punctuation mark. Braille was invented by Louis Braille, a Frenchman who lost his sight as a child. For Helen Keller, learning Braille was a significant step in her education, allowing her to read books and write letters independently.

2. Sign Language

Sign language is a visual language that uses hand shapes, facial expressions, and body movements to communicate. It is used by people who are deaf or hard of hearing. American Sign Language (ASL) is one of the most commonly used sign languages in the United States. Helen Keller learned sign language as part of her communication methods, enabling her to express her thoughts and understand others.

3. Tactile Sign Language

Tactile sign language is a method of communication used by individuals who are both deaf and blind. It involves feeling the hand signs of a communication partner by placing one's hands over theirs. This allowed Helen Keller to understand what was being said to her by feeling the movements and shapes of the signs made by her teacher, Anne Sullivan.

4. Finger Spelling

Finger spelling is a part of sign language where each letter of the alphabet is represented by a specific hand shape. This method is often used to spell out names, places, or words that do not have a specific sign. Helen Keller relied on finger spelling as one of her primary methods of communication. Anne Sullivan would spell words into Helen's hand, allowing her to understand spoken language.

5. Advocacy

Advocacy involves actively supporting a cause or proposal. It includes speaking out on issues, raising awareness, and working towards positive change. Helen Keller was a dedicated advocate for the rights of people with disabilities. Her efforts helped to improve education, accessibility, and opportunities for individuals with disabilities around the world.

6. Disability Rights

Disability rights refer to the civil rights of individuals with disabilities. These rights ensure that people with disabilities have equal access to education, employment, transportation, and other areas of life. Helen Keller's work significantly contributed to the disability rights movement, promoting policies and laws that protect and empower people with disabilities.

7. Perseverance

Perseverance means continuing to work towards a goal despite facing difficulties or setbacks. Helen Keller's life exemplifies perseverance. Despite losing her sight and hearing at a young age, she remained determined to learn, communicate, and advocate for others. Her perseverance enabled her to overcome immense challenges and achieve extraordinary accomplishments.

8. Sensory Experience

Sensory experience involves the way we perceive the world through our senses: sight, hearing, touch, taste, and smell. Helen Keller's sensory experiences were unique because she relied heavily on her senses of touch, taste, and smell. These senses helped her understand and interact with her environment, compensating for her lack of sight and hearing.

9. Inclusion

Inclusion refers to creating environments where all individuals, regardless of their abilities, can participate fully and equally. Helen Keller's advocacy promoted the inclusion of people with disabilities in all aspects of society, from education to employment. Her work aimed to ensure that everyone had the opportunity to contribute and belong.

10. Education

Education is the process of receiving or giving systematic instruction, especially at a school or university. For Helen Keller, education was a transformative experience. With the help of Anne Sullivan and other educators, Helen learned to read, write, and communicate, unlocking her potential and allowing her to make significant contributions to society.

11. Empathy

Empathy is the ability to understand and share the feelings of another person. Helen Keller's experiences fostered a deep sense of empathy, which drove her advocacy work. She understood the challenges faced by people with disabilities and dedicated her life to improving their lives through empathy and action.

12. Communication Devices

Communication devices are tools that help people with disabilities communicate. These can include Braille writers, speech-to-text software, and other assistive technologies. Helen Keller used various communication devices throughout her life to read, write, and interact with others. These devices played a crucial role in her education and advocacy work.

13. Independence

Independence refers to the ability to live and function without relying on others. Helen Keller's education and determination helped her achieve a high level of independence. Despite her disabilities, she was able to communicate, travel, and advocate for herself and others. Her story inspires people to strive for independence, regardless of their challenges.

14. Motivation

Motivation is the reason or reasons one has for acting or behaving in a particular way. Helen Keller's motivation came from her desire to learn, communicate, and help others. Her inner drive pushed her to overcome obstacles and achieve her goals, serving as a powerful example of how motivation can lead to extraordinary accomplishments.

15. Rehabilitation

Rehabilitation involves the process of restoring someone to health or normal life through training and therapy after illness or injury. Helen Keller benefited from various forms of rehabilitation, including learning to communicate through tactile methods and Braille. Rehabilitation played a significant role in her ability to interact with the world and achieve her goals.

16. Inspirational

Something that is inspirational provides motivation or encouragement to do or feel something, especially to do something creative or beneficial. Helen Keller's life and achievements are incredibly inspirational. Her story encourages others to overcome their own challenges and make a positive impact in their communities.

17. Adaptation

Adaptation refers to the process of adjusting to new conditions or environments. Helen Keller had to adapt to her loss of sight and hearing by learning new ways to communicate and interact with the world. Her ability to adapt was crucial to her success and serves as a powerful lesson in resilience and flexibility.

18. Social Justice

Social justice is the concept of fair and just relations between the individual and society. It involves the distribution of wealth, opportunities, and privileges within a society. Helen Keller was a strong advocate for social justice, working to ensure that people with disabilities had equal rights and opportunities.

resources

1. Helen Keller Kids Museum Online (Helen Keller Foundation)

This interactive website is designed specifically for kids. It includes a virtual tour of Helen Keller's home, fun facts, and interactive activities that make learning about Helen's life both educational and entertaining.

2. American Foundation for the Blind (AFB) – Helen Keller Archive

The AFB has a comprehensive online archive dedicated to Helen Keller. It includes letters, photographs, and other primary sources that provide a deep dive into her life and work. There are also educational resources and lesson plans available for teachers and parents.

3. PBS LearningMedia – Helen Keller

PBS offers a range of educational videos and resources about Helen Keller. These materials are designed for classroom use but are also great for individual learning. The videos include dramatizations of key moments in Helen's life, interviews with historians, and more.

4. National Women's History Museum – Helen Keller

The National Women's History Museum has an online exhibit dedicated to Helen Keller. It includes a timeline of her life, photographs, and educational resources that provide a comprehensive overview of her achievements and legacy.

5. Library of Congress – Helen Keller Collection

The Library of Congress hosts a digital collection of Helen Keller's papers and artifacts. This extensive archive includes correspondence, manuscripts, and photographs, offering a detailed look at her life and work. The site also includes educational resources for students and teachers.

Multimedia Resources

1. "The Miracle Worker" (Movie)

This classic film dramatizes the early years of Helen Keller and her relationship with Anne Sullivan. Watching this movie can provide kids with a vivid and emotional understanding of the challenges Helen faced and the breakthroughs she achieved with Anne's help.

2. "Helen Keller: The Story of My Life" (Documentary)

This documentary offers a comprehensive look at Helen Keller's life, featuring interviews, archival footage, and insights from historians. It's an excellent resource for kids to see real footage and learn from experts about Helen's impact.

3. Audiobooks

Listening to audiobooks about Helen Keller can be a great way for kids to learn while engaging their auditory senses. Many of the books mentioned above are available in audiobook format, providing an alternative way to explore Helen's story.

Educational Activities and Projects

1. Braille Activities

Introduce kids to Braille by using resources like

Braille alphabet cards and worksheets. Kids can learn to write their names in Braille and even create simple messages. This hands-on activity helps them understand how Helen Keller read and wrote.

2. Sign Language Lessons

Teaching kids basic sign language can be both fun and educational. There are numerous online resources and apps that offer tutorials on American Sign Language (ASL). Learning a few key phrases or the alphabet in ASL can give kids a sense of how Helen Keller communicated.

3. Sensory Exploration Projects

Activities that focus on sensory experiences can help kids appreciate Helen Keller's unique way of interacting with the world. Blindfolded activities, tactile exploration with different textures, and taste and smell challenges can provide insight into how Helen used her senses of touch, taste, and smell.

4. Virtual Tours

Many museums and historical sites offer virtual tours that can be accessed online. Taking a virtual tour of Helen Keller's birthplace, Ivy Green, or the Perkins School for the Blind can provide a visual and interactive way to learn about her life and environment.

5. Creative Writing and Art Projects

Encourage kids to write stories or create artwork inspired by Helen Keller's life. They can imagine what it would be like to meet Helen or write about how her story inspires them. Art projects might include drawing scenes from her life or creating posters that highlight her achievements.

Connecting with Helen's Legacy

1. Fundraising and Awareness Campaigns

Organize a fundraising event or awareness campaign to support organizations that continue Helen Keller's work, such as Helen Keller International or the American Foundation for the Blind. Kids can participate in bake sales, charity runs, or create informational posters to raise awareness about disability rights.

2. Volunteering

Encourage kids to volunteer with local organizations that support people with disabilities. Volunteering can provide hands-on experience and help kids develop empathy and a deeper understanding of the challenges faced by individuals with disabilities.

3. Creating Accessibility Projects

Kids can work on projects that promote accessibility in their own communities. This might include advocating for Braille signs in public places, creating accessible resources for school events, or designing inclusive playgrounds. These projects help kids apply what they've learned about Helen Keller to make a positive impact in their surroundings.

Exploring these resources and activities allows kids to gain a deeper understanding of Helen Keller's life and the values she stood for. Through books, websites, multimedia, and hands-on projects, they can learn about resilience, advocacy, and the importance of inclusivity, all while being inspired by Helen Keller's incredible journey.

Made in the USA
Middletown, DE
20 January 2025

69870382R00080